The Refined Being

From the Fire of Adversity to One's Greater Purpose

Star K. Edwards

Copywriting By: Venus Edwards at LadyLiterary.com

Library of Congress Cataloging – in- Publication Data has been applied for.

ISBN: 979-8-9868377-7-2

PRINTED IN THE UNITED STATES OF AMERICA.

Acknowledgements

1st To God "Yahweh" and my Lord and Savior Jesus Christ "Yeshua" Who I Prayed Would Guide Me With The Holy Spirit "'Ha Ruach Ha Kodesh" In Writing The Words Which Need To Be In This Book.

To My Two Sweet Little Boys, My Sons Trustyn "Taleio" & Sebastian, mommy is so happy & blessed to have a new refined life because of you and for you. I am now building a great legacy for you, my loves to continue on. I love you both with every ounce of my being.

To My Mother, Jessie thank you for encouraging me to have a relationship with God and for sacrificing so much for me and my sisters. Thank you also for giving us a good education and the arts. Congratulations on telling your story in the multi-author book and I look forward to seeing your spiritual book being published.

To My Father, Kisiar (R.I.P.) thank you for being a dad who stayed in our lives, for having a relationship with us, for your encouragement and late-night talks. Thank you for sharing your love of music with me. I miss you daddy.

To My Sister, Venus for being a sweet loving sister and

for authoring the beautiful poem inspired by my life and published in this book, "Refined out of the Rough." Thank you for also copywriting this book for me under your business.

To My Sister, Jessica Shaday for being a lovely sister and for referring me to your publisher.

To my grandparents (R.I.P.) and to my grandma Pearline "Dear" (R.I.P.) who I enjoyed spending a lot of time with.

To my uncle Alfred "Jerome" for supporting me in times I needed support and for being a good role model.

To my cousin Wendy Gladney for being inspiring and for touching many people's lives for the better with your work.

To my friends, Dominique Moye and Catrina Gaston who are also recent authors, who encouraged me through this journey & being there for one another during the pandemic.

To my friends, Larisa Eiley & Tanya James for us also being there for one another, especially during the pandemic.

To my friend Rebecca Barlow (Reba) (R.I.P.) thank you for being a great light on this earth, for coming to see my baby boys after their births, and for praying with me w/the prayer team to find the root of my hurt so I can refine myself.

To my other family, friends including internationally, to my foreign exchange students, my bible study & prayer teams, including my prayer partners in Paris, France. To friends I've met within church, Randy & Cheryl Lee and

Pastor Manoj & Suzy Mathai to other beautiful spirited people who have been encouraging and are bright lights. To therapists I've worked with, my previous social worker at UCLA campus (R.I.P.). To my UCLA community, especially at UCLA Family Housing University Village, including my friend's Nicole Lombard and Ana-Lisa Clark Mullen & family who were my support especially when my sons were babies.

To my narcissistic abuse survivor's community tribe including Dana Morningstar-Thrive After Abuse who was the 1st youtuber which helped bring me into awareness of my life & helped to save my life and refine it. To youtuber Angie Atkinson (R.I.P.) who was nearly the 2nd youtuber who truly helped my life. To the most recent youtuber Telsha Edenburg-The Tea on NPD & Relationships who has done the same and speaks more on the spiritual aspects of narcissistic abuse and our lives. To a whole host of narcissistic abuse awareness youtubers who've helped me refine my life, my whole being, and who have been so instrumental to my healing. To Bree Bonchay, the founder of world narcissistic abuse awareness day for also helping save lives.

To my publisher, who has been so patient with me during this process and allowed me to continue on to write and publish way over a year past the deadline and to everyone who helped me bring this book to life, including Christian Cuan who with my vision, helped me create the most beautiful and astounding book cover, which is now also my logo.

To my new company, "Refined Being Media, Arts, &

Star K. Edwards

Communications for the many true inspiring stories I'm starting to tell for other people through media, arts, communications, and sociocultural visual anthropology.

Letter From an Empath…

While I love to help others, I am not responsible for fixing your life or catering to your toxicity. I am not responsible for managing your triggers, walking on eggshells or telling you what you want to hear in order to keep the peace. I am not your emotional punching bag nor am I your emotional sponge. I do not exist for your pleasure or as a site for your projected pain. My responsibility is to myself — to be my own person and stay true to myself — to heal my own wounds, manage my own triggers, and engage in self-care so that I can give to others authentically without depleting myself in the process. My responsibility is to maintain healthy boundaries — especially with those who are unhealthy.

Shahida Arabi

Refined, Out of the Rough

Written by Venus Y. Edwards
Inspired by Star K. Edwards' New Refined Life

One day, realizing that two months has been burning
into three years of my life,
Which it was now nearly four decades of living life,
What else could I say?
Ignited within me a fire they tried to burn me with.
Blazing so hot till my feet could no longer take the
candlewick.
Melted the ink that formed significant adversity,
My journey through these obstacles was so ocean deep.
They thirsted and hungered, feeding off of me.
Trying to draw away all my positive energy.
To only leave me skinless and bone dry.
Chucked me into a lake flowing with consistent tides.
That's then where my new life began.
Now emerging to the top only to see the blazing sun,
Crying out from the battle, "Yes! We won!"
Prevailing for my children and the generations to come.
A diamond doesn't shine till it's been through the
rough.
They thought I wouldn't survive it.
Now to be inspired, here I am standing, a refined being
in full attire.

Star K. Edwards

Being on the mountaintop dwelling in God's Glory,
Can't stop me. I'm telling my life story!
So, brace yourself for this bright star diamond you're now seeing.
Yes, I survived! I am a Refined Being!

Table Of Contents

Introduction   15

Chapter I:

Refining My Consciousness and Self-Awareness   17

Chapter II:

Refining My Family, Childhood, and Teen Years   21

Chapter III:

Refining My Accomplishments, Favor, and Setbacks in
My 20s   39

Chapter IV:

Refining the Passing of My Father; My Late 20s and
Early 30s   51

Chapter V:

Refining Narcissistic Abuse and the Future Faking of
Narcissism   73

Chapter VI:

Refining Church Hurt. Oh My!   91

Chapter VII:

Refining My Motherhood—the Happiness and the
Struggles   103

Chapter VIII:

Refining My Hardest Life Decision   119

Chapter IX:

Refining Myself Throughout the Pandemic—Hypocrisy
of Country, Race, Culture, and Spirituality   129

Chapter X:

Refining a Brand-New Me; Love, Light, & More God   141

Extra Self-Reflection Note Pages

For My Readers to Reflect on Your Own Story & For
You to Also Become a Refined Being   153

The Refined Being

From the Fire of Adversity to
One's Greater Purpose

Introduction

"How does one become a butterfly? You must want to fly so much that you are willing to give up being a caterpillar."

— *Trina Paulus*

I have always been well accomplished, a high achiever, and favored by many people most of my life. Also, once I set a goal, nothing can stop me from achieving it! I persevere until the end, no matter the circumstances. I've been blessed to be a gifted person. At the same time, I was broken somewhere inside my being and did not know where the brokenness stemmed from. Many remarkable things happened both for me and to me. That is until I started allowing toxic people into my life. When my father, mother, sisters, and other family

Star K. Edwards

members began experiencing similar toxic situations and people in their lives, I realized some generational chains needed to be broken and environments needed to be changed. In this book, *The Refined Being*, I will share my experiences with toxic people and how their toxicity almost led to my destruction. I will also help you as a reader to digest your own life and to see how you can break intergenerational chains to thrive for oneself, for one's children and for future generations to come. I asked myself, why was I so fragmented to allow these life-altering experiences that nearly destroyed me? In this book, I will also demonstrate the great perseverance I had despite tremendous obstacles. I was placed in burning fires but came out "shining like God's diamond!"

By reading this book, you will also learn how to reflect on your life, do some soul-searching, and use these methods to refine yourself. Adversities didn't destroy me, and I now know who I am. I'm shining on that mountain top with God's glory radiating down on and within me. I'm giving Him all the glory with all of my being, The Refined Being! We are all spiritual beings having a human experience!

"BELIEVE IN YOURSELF AND ALL THAT YOU ARE. KNOW THAT THERE IS SOMETHING INSIDE YOU THAT IS GREATER THAN ANY OBSTACLE."

Chapter I:

Refining My Conscious and Self-Awareness

Consciousness — the state of being awake and aware of one's surroundings. It can also be a state of being painfully aware of and sensitive to the world. Conscious is the awareness that something is happening or is the normal state of being awake. It is also used to describe someone coming into oneself after passing out. This was me—that was and *is* my story.

God, what is going on? I would ask, crying out to Him from the depths of my soul. I cried so hard I thought I would bust a brain vessel. *Where am I? Am I still on Earth? Are people here on Earth just that evil?*

Now, I am not perfect by any means. Still, I have

never intentionally tried to cause harm to people just for the sake of causing harm—not mentally, emotionally, physically, spiritually, or otherwise. When I was younger and needed some healing in my life, I do remember a couple of people who I will now apologize to for hurting. I pray they will accept my apology. On the other end, I've been through a series of circumstances and crossed paths with people who caused me much harm. The icing on the cake was coming to the realization that the person I had vowed to create a life with was only concerned with self. It was "I" and not "we" when it came to us. I came to the awareness that this was all connected somehow. My mistakes, circumstances, and pain were all connected— a whirlwind of trauma and seeking love.

Why was it so hard to get something as simple as love? Why would I give and give of myself but not receive anything in return but a lot of heartache? The heartaches grew increasingly stronger each time I tried it with someone new. What was I doing wrong? What was it about me that I couldn't be loved back? Some qualities of love are putting others' needs before one's own, being a part of a team, and working together gracefully. Love makes you feel content, not anxious, and is synonymous with empathy. Why was I associating with people who couldn't love? Once I vowed to go full force with love, why did I experience the ultimate hate for it?

These were the questions I asked God "Yahweh"! I screamed out to Him with all of my being! Why did I keep making these same mistakes? The answer was that I needed to give God all of me and experience His love––to seek Him more spiritually and less of what I wanted in the flesh. Before I realized these things, I contemplated freeing myself from the overbearing misery. It felt like the walls of life were crumbling all around me, and no one tried to rescue me! I heard a whispering voice faintly but could not make out the words. *God, is that you? Are you there? If so, I am right here on bended knees.*

With my tears all dried out, it felt like I was sinking. I saw the faces of the people who tried to destroy me—specifically the recent face, which was fixed with a smirk of laughter from my pain! It was just me alone in this with my baby boy and another baby boy on the way, and now the same people who tried to destroy, manipulate, and gaslight me wanted me to go insane. In desperation, I reached up to grab what I thought was a helping hand, only to find someone pouring more sand on top of me.

Chapter II:

Refining My Family, Childhood, and Teen Years

History. Your story is your story. Your story made you; it is a part of you. However, how your life began doesn't have to be your future or ending. Some people tend to think what they've been through is what will continue, but you can change your story. Growing up has built you into the person you are today. Once you're older, you can take the good parts of your experiences, use them to be a great human being, and turn whatever started as bad into something good. Everyone has a story, and here's mine.

I grew up with incredibly attractive parents. My mother was seventeen when she met my father, who was about nine years her senior. While my mom grew up in a small town in East Texas, my dad was raised in Los Angeles, California. Both have Creole roots, with my dad having a Creole Louisiana background and, from what I've been told, being descendants from family in the Caribbean. Creole describes descendants of French or Spanish colonists with a mixed racial heritage— French or Spanish mixed with African American and/or Native American.

When my mother was a little girl, she grew up amid the Civil Rights movement and was a part of some of the first groups of children who had to integrate with people of European descent in Texas. To this day, she still tells this story because it profoundly touched her life in many ways. My maternal grandmother grew up in Texas, but something occurred that caused her to flee from East Texas to Southern California with her children, who ranged in age from twelve years old to near adulthood. No one has ever told the whole story of why she up and quickly fled one day with mostly just the clothes on her back. She left her husband—my grandfather—and moved with her children to Los Angeles, California, where her eldest daughter had recently resided. My mother still hasn't gotten over having to leave her home during her senior year of high school, where she was an honor student and involved in different positive activities with her childhood friends. My mother never imagined she would be picked up after school one day and find herself fleeing across the U.S. without any notice.

The Refined Being

When they arrived in Los Angeles, it was during the mid-1970s when crack cocaine and weapons were purposely placed in neighborhoods of color. This was a culture shock for the family. My grandmother, my mother, and her siblings were what you might call "country folks," having grown up in a small town. Now they were living in inner-city L.A. amongst drugs and gang wars. My mother was terrified. Her entire world came tumbling down all at once.

Now seventeen, my mother was growing into her womanly beauty. One day while walking down the street, this handsome bi-racial-looking guy came riding up alongside her on his bicycle with hair flowing all over his head. That handsome man was my father. My parents eventually became an item; he was the person my mother leaned on while trying to adjust to the traumatic inner-city Los Angeles culture. Unfortunately, her siblings were having a challenging time adjusting and eventually started getting into trouble.

My dad would help my mother and at times would be there for her family as well. He had recently returned home from the military (army) after being forced to fight in the Vietnam war. My dad was drafted when he was around eighteen years old and forced to go into battle as a teen. I was told that after seeing one of his close friends perish, he experienced a mental breakdown and was discharged from the military. Before meeting my mother, my father had recently divorced a lady with whom he had a little girl. Not long after, he and my mom met and became each other's love and support.

Star K. Edwards

My mother eventually graduated her senior year in Los Angeles, moved in with my father, and they fell in love. They loved the parties and dancing of the 1970s, and the fashion they wore with the beautiful Afros and bell bottoms was out of this world. They were living like hippies and free. These were the Soul Train days when Black music rocked the world—from jazz to the doo-wop era to Motown, the black influence on rock n roll, funk, jazz, and more. I'm also like a music historian and performing artist, so I speak a lot about music. The kings and queens of music were Black people, and most of the ones who dominated music, who were not Black had many times been musically influenced by Black people. Or should I say melanated people with the skin color of brown, tan, red, etc. But that's another story for another chapter.

When my mother was around twenty-one years old and my father about thirty, they gave birth to me and eventually got married. They started out happy in their relationship, but things eventually turned south. My father did not want to settle down. He wanted to keep partying. Having left work at the Long Beach Shipyard, he was a veteran with much time on his hands. So, he became an entrepreneur, opening the Magic Car Wash, where he provided car detailing services. He loved cars, especially antiques. My father owned approximately four antique vintage cars from the 1930s and 1940s, including a Rolls Royce. He loved chauffeuring other people and us, his children around in his antique cars. By this time, my mother had finished business school, worked at USC, a major cosmetic department store, and eventually worked at the Watts Health Foundation. She was now a young mother and getting help from my grandmother.

My father liked to have company over to the house often, both men and women friends. My mother went through so much trying to get my dad to stop partying and take care of the family. My parents had purchased a beautiful Spanish-style home, which my mom didn't get a chance to enjoy because of my father's immaturity—doing what he wanted to do without much consideration for becoming a man and to take care of responsibility. Believing things would get better between her and my father, my mother gave birth to my sister, Venus. People always knew us by Star and Venus. We grew up as babies and young girls in the 1980s and were given these celestial names.

My parents fought a lot. Eventually, they separated, and we moved out of our house and into an apartment a few blocks away next door to my grandmother. It was in the middle of one of the worst gang-war-infested streets. This was also where there were pimps and prostitutes. My mother sheltered my sister and me, making us stay indoors most of the time, and we were put into private schooling away from the riff-raff during the day. My mother sacrificed so much to have us in Christian and Catholic private schools. We sometimes were allowed to play in the yard but would have to run inside whenever the gangs started shooting. As I mentioned, the country people, my family were now in the middle of this gang war and had no idea it would be like this moving from a small Texas town, even though there was a different type of violence hidden there. But it's what my family could afford at the time in Los Angeles.

I loved Christian school and eventually moved over to attending Catholic School. I had always loved school and had always been an honor student. I loved that my dad stayed in our lives even though he and my mom ended up getting a divorce. Every day my dad would take us to school and call to make sure we were safe. My mom worked a lot and was always upset about how her life turned out. As if the stress of trying to make sure my sisters and I had everything we needed wasn't enough, my mother's siblings always seemed to try to destroy her.

I had to step up at a young age to take care of me and my sisters. I guess my mother felt I was mature enough. As a result, I grew up fast, taking on the responsibility since I was the oldest sibling in our house. Whenever we went to my dad's, our original house, I would see my dad's first-born daughter with whom I had a relationship until my adult years. She went through a traumatic childhood and life, which she never healed from, and took things out on others, including me. I finally decided to let toxicity go. I would eventually go through a series of hurt and pain from hurt people throughout my life and had to refine myself fully from it.

Some things changed heading into my teen years. My mother sacrificed working many years at the United

States Postal Service to purchase another home, but this time she did it on her own. That was a tremendous accomplishment for a divorced mother. My mother was now pregnant after a decade with my second sister, Jessica, whom she named close to her name like a juniorette. I was so happy to meet Jessica the day my mom brought her home from the hospital and be her big sister. It was now my mother and her three girls in our new home. My mother tried to help her brothers by giving them a place to stay in our back house and to help them better their lives. In return, they tried destroying her, her property, etc. She tried to have a good relationship with her sisters, but they had a lot of toxic behaviors as well. Her siblings envied her because she always worked hard to have a better life and tried to have a prayer life. I believe her continuing to stay around those narcissistic family members affected her, which then affected us—her children. They still at times have crazy-making activities going on. This was a family dynamic and dysfunctional cycle that I would eventually figure out and break.

My mother did well not to fully become like her siblings, but due to their upbringing and my mother not realizing the cycle fully that she needed to break, there were some emotional wounds she passed on to my sisters and me. I appreciate my mother so much for all her sacrifices. She may not have been emotionally healthy while raising us or into our adulthood, but she worked hard for us. No one is perfect. Unfortunately, those emotional wounds that my mother's family and others created within her affected us. I felt broken as a child, invalidated, and devalued. Most things I said were wrong; most things I thought or did were wrong. I couldn't speak about almost anything. My feelings did not matter. I wasn't supposed to have feelings or express them. My sisters and I felt unseen, unheard, etc. I know she did the best she could. She was hurt, and hurt people hurt other people. Maybe it was unintentional due to generational trauma, mental health issues which needed to be addressed, etc. We were somewhat emotionally and mentally damaged even into adulthood from the family dynamic and caretakers not caring how another person is feeling or hurting, but proceed to pour salt in the continuous wounds. I'm glad that things are a little better these days, but still needs work.

Even though I had my little sisters with me while growing up, I felt so alone at times. I felt like there were no adults around many times—no one to talk to or get advice from. Getting advice was recurrently, to be emotionally abused and if you reacted to it, you were gaslit, made to feel like something was wrong with you. Whenever certain adult(s) were around, they were not really there and seemed to get easily triggered, becoming angry immediately and almost daily. It was a crazy-making unlovable environment because of one's hurt and pain. This eventually led to me looking for love and acceptance in absolutely all the wrong places.

I had a culture shock in my teen years. My mom could not afford to keep her two oldest daughters in private school any longer, only the youngest one, so I ended up attending a rough inner-city public high school. There was one good thing about that school—it had the top music program in Los Angeles with a famous producer as our music teacher Mr. Reggie Andrews who recently passed away (R.I.P.). I made the best of my time there at my high school, even though it was hard to make friends. The positive point about this time of my life, I was able to get more involved in performing arts which from then on until adulthood became my outlet to express myself, especially since I was not able to express my feelings, even positively within my home and also around people in a broken community. I was able to do this within the arts. This is why to this day, I still have a deep passion and love for the arts!

Before going to this school, I had to try out at the adjacent middle school for a few months. There was a girl in the eighth grade who could not read and had no friends. Realizing I had an empathetic and empathic side, I took time out of recess and lunch breaks to teach her how to read. I don't know if teachers knew what we were doing. I have and had a heart for helping people and just wanted her to succeed. Many years later, when we were adults, I ran into her. She was homeless and mentally ill. I tried helping her again; that was the last time I saw her.

When I started high school, I succeeded in school. Because of my foundation in Christian and Catholic private schooling and my love for school and education overall, I excelled in the public school. I was a leader in my school. I was an honor student, I voted as the Director of Publicity for the student council, started as a flag girl in the band and became a cheerleader, and was in the high school sorority called "Phenomenal Ladies". I was in the business program which helped prepare students to apply for work after high school and learned to type 70 words per minute. I was in a singing group with the now-famous actor and singer Tyrese Gibson who starred in the movie "Fast & Furious, Transformers, etc." and he would come to my home after school to practice on our piano while we waited to be picked up to perform at various events as teens. At this time, I also joined another weekend performing arts group in which I eventually performed in Europe at the age of turning seventeen (17) years old. Because of all the work I did in my high school and community, I was given an award from the California State Assembly and had a story written about me in the local newspaper by the time I was fifteen years old. At the age of fifteen (15), I also won the Miss Teen Los Angeles title and competed in the Miss Teen California Pageant with other accomplished teens from all over the state of California.

Even though I grew up in a neighborhood in which most people called a Black and Latino community of what people may call many lower working-class individuals, I was well accomplished and moving upward to success in the midst of. I was beyond ambitious and always had the tenacity to succeed, even in some of the worst circumstances. I am glad my mother instilled in me the importance of education, allowed me to pursue my passion in the arts, and being well-rounded. My dad was supportive and encouraged me to do my best. I made homecoming princess one year in high school, and my dad chauffeured me in one of his antique vintage cars in the homecoming parade. My dad also took me to my first concert when I was just eleven (11) years old to see my favorite boy band group, "New Kids on the Block" who I still enjoy seeing to this day. I wanted to marry the youngest member of the group, Joey McIntyre when I was a pre-teen/young teen. My second favorite singer of the group at that time was and is the lead vocalist, Jordan Knight. Laugh out loud. My dad seemed to enjoy their concert just as much as I did. We had an awesome father/daughter time together. These are some of my greatest memories with my dad. My mother helped prepare me for the Miss Teen California Scholarship Pageant and helped me get sponsors. This is a fond memory, as well, regarding my mother and my father. Even though I have had my difficulties with my parents, they had to grow, too. Knowing I had to do my part as a child, I tried hard to be that perfect child. I do appreciate them for the contributions they have given me and my sisters.

Around sixteen (16) years old, I soon discovered a very tall light skin boy with green eyes who would become my high school boyfriend. I always seemed to have had some sort of puppy love. I loved the idea of love and being in love. My first puppy love was in grade school and then heading to middle school, there was puppy love with a boy from El Salvador. In high school, this boyfriend was on the basketball team, and I was a cheerleader. He had an interesting family, to say the least. His father was over controlling and he was a parent who everyone knew at the school. I had a cousin who also attended the school. My paternal grandfather, who was her caretaker at the time, sent my cousin to my school because I was doing well there. I was happy to finally have someone to be with at school. Even better, she was my cousin. I thought it would be even better to have family with me and we could be there for one another.

On her first day starting at my school, I waited at the front gate for her so I could greet her and show her around. As soon as she came in, she rolled her eyes at me and acted as if she did not want to be bothered. From that day on, she became one of my bullies at school. I was bullied for what kids said, speaking too white and smiling too much. You were supposed to be rough at a so-called rough school. That wasn't me; I was never rough. When my boyfriend and I broke up, he bullied me along with his sister on the girls' basketball team and my cousin on the same team, which as I mentioned was my other bully. I eventually found a friend in my last year of school who later turned out not to be a loyal friend in our adult years. Like some of my other so-called friends in the past, she had some sort of jealousy and wanted to compete with me when I was not even aware there was a competition. In regards to my cousin, she apologized to me when we became of age and I appreciated her for this. This is what we are supposed to do in our lives with the people we are associated with and come across. It is about forgiving and asking for forgiveness.

I skipped the 11th grade and was a senior at sixteen years old. Yes, I had a good head on my shoulders, but again, I was missing full emotional love from my parents. I also started to take some of my pain out on my sister who was born after me when I started puberty, but later apologized to her when I became of age. I realized I was starting to have some anxiety and didn't know what was happening. My father could have pitched in more, my mother was tired and hurt being around toxic people, and the anger continued. Many occurrences that happened to her were taken out on us. She seemed not to be able to help it. Again, I was devalued and invalidated about mostly everything. She was sad due to the continuous abuse from her family and the abandonment and abuse of men who left her, making her a single parent. Again, she worked hard to give us the best, and we saw or spoke to our dad every day, but he was more like a friend to joke around with. I wish my dad would've been mature enough to sit us down and teach us some things about people and relationships. He showed us attention as long as it did not interfere with one of his girlfriends. This was another situation that led me to start seeking love and acceptance in all the wrong places.

I truly believe things would've been better if we were all in the same household and working together as a family. Since I never felt fully loved and could not

33

communicate my feelings without being met with anger, I started accepting fake love from men. Parents set up how their children will relate to people in future relationships. It's about a child's programming. For example, if a parent is abusive, chances are the child will become an abuser or get involved in relationships with abusers if the cycle is not broken. Also, some of our parents need healing. However, a person must first acknowledge that they need to heal and then take the necessary steps.

At seventeen (17) years old, I went to Europe (Copenhagen, Denmark) for a few weeks to perform in a musical theater in a stage play. I was so glad my mom agreed to let me go at the last minute. My mentors asked my mother for weeks in allowing me to get my United States passport and to go with the other performers so we all could perform together. I stayed with a family as an international student and performer. After performing in musical theater in Europe and mentoring younger kids, I finally came back to the States. That's when I noticed my body had blossomed. My looks changed, and I started receiving unbelievable attention from all the wrong ailments in the wrong environments. While in Europe, a European Danish boy in Denmark said he was in love with me. He would give me teddy bears and other little gifts and follow me around before I came back to the States. Could he have been a good person to get to know better? Maybe so. I should've probably considered staying in Denmark and not kept Los Angeles my home. It was such an awesome time.

Looking back on my childhood, I thank God for the good times and tough times. The good times felt great, but the tough times helped to build me up to be strong. After this chapter in my life, I refined my being by overcoming the trials of my childhood/teen years and thanked God for all the blessings He has given me.

Reflection: Get a journal or start here. Think of your childhood and teen years. What were some of the good memories? What are some of the things you need to heal from and release? Think deeply: Are there any generational cycles that need to be broken? Who do you need to forgive? Who do you need to apologize to? Write them down along with anything else that comes to your mind pertaining to this topic.

Star K. Edwards

_____

_____

_____

_____

_____

_____

_____

_____

_____

_____

_____

_____

_____

_____

_____

_____

_____

_____

Star K. Edwards

_____

_____

_____

_____

_____

_____

_____

_____

_____

_____

_____

_____

_____

_____

_____

_____

_____

_____

Chapter III:

Refining My Accomplishments, Favor, and Setbacks in My 20s

After returning from performing in Europe, I needed direction and some support to continue in performing arts. My mother tried dating again but ended up with a man who became abusive. She didn't know how to cope with being inflicted with so much hurt and pain. As a result, there was much crazymaking in the home. It also affected her ability to see, value, or communicate normally with me, which I acknowledged because of this, I could not communicate normally back. So, I started my first real job at Bank of America at eighteen and moved out into my own apartment. When I was a kid, I used to admire the intelligent-looking women in the bank dressed in their professional clothing in skirts, blouses, suits, and pantyhose with heels. My mom taught my sisters and I on how to dress and to always be well put together, and I thank her for that. To this day, I dress well, and my mother dresses very nicely, too.

Eventually, I became one of the young ladies working in banking and moved up quickly in the industry. I did have to get a second job as a hostess at a local restaurant to pay bills, but my heart was always thinking of the arts. I was finally able to express myself through the arts. I would always sing and dance, etc. while working my jobs. My co-workers knew I loved to perform, and they enjoyed seeing it. I wanted so badly to be back performing and working in the arts. I just needed to be patient.

Another goal of mine was to attend college. I had been a high achiever and an honor student, so I was accepted to universities but opted to pursue my career in the entertainment industry since I was connected to a few producers etc. in the industry who were sending me out on auditions. My performances in Europe were even a connection with Paramount & Sony Pictures, who funded me for Europe to perform at the age of seventeen. I also received a scholarship to attend the California Institute of the Arts, one of the top performing arts schools leading to the film and television industries. I attended the summer before, and after getting my apartment and working two plus jobs, I started losing momentum while pursuing my dreams. I didn't stay focused; my new focus became love. This eventually became my downfall.

While working, I started attending the local community college, El Camino College. That's where I met my college boyfriend, Christopher Tyler. He was nice-looking and very sweet. He would be the only boyfriend who ever fully treated me well. My parents liked him, and we were always together. I dated him right before I got my first apartment. We would go to class and hang out in the local park. I was in love; he was in love. But then, one day, I don't know what got into me. I didn't want to be with him any longer. I broke up with him and broke his heart. Years later, I ran into his sister, who told me that he couldn't eat or sleep for weeks when I broke up with him. She said he also started some other unhealthy habits due to being depressed over me. When I ran into him many years later, he was a happily married man with children. We never talked again after that time. I wanted to explore the temptations of the world while at the same time on a mission looking for love but finding it in all the wrong places. Looking back, I should've possibly stayed with Christopher, but it was young love.

There was a time I was at church about two to three days a week in bible study and rehearsals for the choir and praise team while growing up. I had become a church leader as a child—putting together church programs, teaching the children in Sunday school, and speaking in front of the congregation at a very young age. In my twenties, I started dating guys and found they were nice at first but then would become mean and abusive. I eventually met a guy who came with me to church. We spent a lot of time together, and my pastor liked him, mainly because he gave money to the church. My pastor told us to keep a secret and to get married without telling people until the big wedding, including our parents and family. I don't know why this had to be a secret. I was not pregnant or anything of a tremendous nature. I respected pastors and thought they always knew what was best, until I grew up and became aware that they are just men like everyone else and that some are using the title of pastor to manipulate, control people and to feel superior over others. There are some good pastors who are called by God and there are some who are using the title and are pretending to be of God and are not good people, who are hypocrites, like the Pharisees in the Bible. I grew up under this pastor and found that he wasn't a really good person. He used the opportunity to put together this marriage between us to keep the guy attending his church etc. I was only twenty (20) years old, turning twenty-one (21) at the time, and I thought my pastor meant well by telling me to do this. I wanted love, so I got married. It was like an arranged marriage by my pastor in the Baptist church. I told my parents the day of my wedding before exchanging vows because I could not keep this a secret. I didn't feel my getting married should be kept a secret from them. My mother and father quickly came to the church to witness it.

The guy I married was almost thirty years old and he wanted to find a way to look powerful and have a leadership role. He eventually said he was called to be a minister. He told me to wear big underwear and dresses to my ankles. I was not allowed to wear anything formed fitting. He wanted me to stop wearing my cute little jeans. He didn't want to be intimate either. He used the bible to have complete dominance over me. My pastor went along with him, advising him to do things to disrespect me in the relationship. He baptized me when I was eight (8) years old, and I grew up under his ministry. He was like a godfather to me, so I didn't understand why he would turn on me. It was heartbreaking, and I found myself young and miserable.

My husband at the time started seeing an older woman, someone more of his caliber. There was something sinister about him, her, and most people connected to him. I eventually was glad things finally ended with us, and he married her. My father's first-born daughter became close to my ex, and they got together to do a smear campaign on me. I would live a lot of my life with people getting together to focus on destroying me, even if they didn't like one another, but they connected because I was the focus.

During this time, I started having panic attacks. I would call 911 because I didn't know what was happening. Doctors didn't figure it out for at least a year. This would also be the start of my depression. I felt so lonely. I wanted love; I wanted a partner or at least more love within my family. Around this time, I should have been focusing on school and most importantly growing my relationship stronger with God.

I eventually started trying to have a relationship with

my dad's side of the family. I had not been around my paternal side of the family much while growing up. I didn't know them; they were like strangers. I didn't even know my first cousins' names, which was awful. I had a relationship with my dad but not with his family. He did not go around his family much, and I never knew why. I reached out to them to get to know them. Male cousins would flirt, especially since we seemed to be strangers and hardly saw each other while growing up. It was wrong and extremely toxic. I started spending time with the family, but many of them were not very warm or welcoming to my sisters or me. The only person who seemed family-like was my uncle, which is my father's brother.

Not long after connecting with my father's side, my grandparents' deaths would start—my maternal grandfather first and then my paternal grandfather. Then within two months, both of my grandmothers passed away. Losing my grandparents was tough for me, especially my maternal grandmother which I spent much time with growing up. People mentioned that I seemed to be her favorite granddaughter. When we left our apartment next door to our grandmother to move into our own home, I only saw my grandmother mostly on Sundays when she cooked her fantastic southern dinners. We would go to church together, and she would smile at me from the first pew as I sang in the choir. I would look down at her and smile. She helped my mother, especially when we were young. I was now around twenty-four years old and getting my life on track.

By this time, I had moved up to the management team at Wells Fargo Bank. I was also becoming a known influential community leader throughout Los Angeles. I became a young spokesperson for Wells Fargo Bank and was asked to serve as an advisor and leader on community boards. I have always done very well in my work and with being an influential leader. I found myself speaking on television and radio about what the organizations I worked with were doing in the community, and I became one of the lead organizers of one of the largest annual community day events in Los Angeles. I loved it. I would always be stopped by people in the city who knew who I was and recognized my face. I was like a local celebrity.

I started doing more work in media and for a television firm briefly and became the spokesperson for community day with the mayor, the head sheriff of Los Angeles County, many California politicians, etc. I was invited into many private settings with powerful people. I also worked on the Los Angeles County Sheriff's advisory council to bridge the gap between them and the inner-city community. I would meet at the sheriff's headquarters, and many of the sheriffs would flirt with me. I was always getting hit on in many places. I was not only a people magnet but a male magnet as well. I was young and didn't know who I was or what I had. I seemed confident but had some insecurities. I eventually seemed to have started finding myself a little more.

I was getting many awards at this time for my work

and contributions. I should've been happy. I mostly felt happy but kept falling into depression and dealing with panic attacks. I pulled it together and did the things I needed to do. People counted on me. Eventually, I would fall into a couple more relationships with men who would chase me and be sweet, then turn out to be very sinister. I would always stay too long. I was pregnant, and then I wasn't. I went through so much mentally and alone. I would not listen to my intuition at this time in my life, and I was being reckless. I was still honing my gifts and trying to find who I was. I didn't really know who I was at the time. I wish I had never stayed in those situations long. I wish I would've had more esteem for myself. I had so many positive things happening to me. My downfall was these loser boyfriends and me not knowing the power I had. I needed to find myself and tap into it.

I started acting, singing, dancing, and modeling again in the evenings and on weekends. I loved the stage, and I loved the camera. I even had opportunities to model as a runway model in the Caribbean and traveled throughout many islands, including Puerto Rico, St. Thomas-Virgin Islands, St. Kitts, Aruba, Bahamas, etc. I would eventually win Miss African American Cultural. I felt happy again. Performing Arts, television work, and competing in pageants always brought me back to my happy place. The arts saved my life. At this time, I took a break from my community work and banking work. Instead, I started networking in the entertainment/arts industry.

I connected with celebrity managers and producers who would invite me to celebrities' homes for get-togethers. I thought this was networking, but it was mostly partying with a little networking. I've been to the homes of and hung out with some of the top world celebrities, especially of color, including Prince, Morris Day and The Time, Jaime Foxx, Brandy, Ray J, Serena Williams, Whitney Houston, Bobby Brown, Danny Glover, and Teena Marie to name a few. I was invited to Michael Jackson's Neverland Valley ranch house with my singing, dance, and acting group when he was living, and I invited my mother to hang out with one of her favorite celebrities, Rick James. One day, when my friends and I were with the singer Morris Day from Morris Day & The Time, he told me I was "refined," and that word would stick with me for years. He noticed something special about me and loved my sophistication. I would also be invited out on dates with celebrities, producers, and managers which I will not name. This was a fun time in my life. I knew many other beautiful young women I was told to ask and invite to the celebrity get-togethers. I had some friends who also wanted to be in the industry. We would try to find the best ways to get into the arts industry. I really didn't like the word entertainment. Eventually, we would find out that our education would open up many doors for us and that we would be more respected because of our education. So, we started to put our focus there.

This chapter in my life was a time of finding myself. I refined myself by realizing that something was missing in my twenties (20s), and it was loving me and getting to know myself. I refined myself by gaining more wisdom and knowing the difference between someone who loves me and someone who doesn't. As I approached my 30s, I thought things were getting better, but the next chapter only seemed to get worse on one end and better on the other. The worst end tried to pull on the best end.

Reflection: Think of your 20s. What were or are some of the good memories? What are some of the things you need to heal from and release? Write them down along with anything else that comes to your mind pertaining to this topic.

Star K. Edwards

_____

_____

_____

_____

_____

_____

_____

_____

_____

_____

_____

_____

_____

_____

_____

_____

Chapter IV:

Refining the Passing of My Father; My Late 20s and Early 30s

In my late twenties (20s), I worked again at Wells Fargo Bank, followed up with some media work, and returned to acting in stage plays, mainly in Hollywood, California. I had just come off a military mission, role-playing with the United States Marines for over a year, helping them with training for the Iraq war. I enjoyed that work. That's when I started to fall in love with sociocultural anthropology and combined it with art.

One day, I was working in the bank when a nice-looking, tall, biracial young guy came in looking for me. Ever since I started working at the age of eighteen, I was used to men coming into my jobs looking for me and sending money, flowers, gifts, etc. I had many admirers, and this had become my weakness. People have always admired my brick house body and smile. I had the natural physique and curves that women today get surgeries to achieve. This was one reason I attracted so many men. People have mentioned my magnetism and charm, as well. This was not always a good thing because I attracted all kinds of men, and the not-so-good men were usually more aggressive in hitting on me.

The young man who came into the bank was about six years my junior. I usually dated older men, sometimes way too old, but I thought if I changed my preference, maybe this could work. He seemed to be a good guy, but he lived with his uncle and didn't have much. I enjoyed going places with him and hanging out at his uncle's by the beach daily. His uncle was a police officer, a highway patrol sergeant, to be exact. I dated this boyfriend for about a year and noticed he was drinking a lot. He would get abusive, especially while drinking. Out of nowhere, he would start acting erratically while we were having an enjoyable time. One day, he pushed me off a bicycle when we were bike riding. A nice girl witnessed it and asked if she should call the police, but I told her no. Another time when we were at his home, he ripped my shirt right off of me out of anger. His uncle wasn't there at the time. I never knew where these fits of rage were coming from. Everything seemed to be fine between us other than his drinking. So, I tried to be patient and work with him. I also eventually found myself not having many boundaries. I thought at the time if I pleased people and did whatever it took to keep them happy, that they would be happy. Little did I know. I learned the hard way.

When he was caught drinking on the job, I helped him find another job. I created a resume, scouted jobs for him, and helped him get into school. I had always tried to put a lot into others and focused on myself last. People who were users saw this in me and took full advantage. I had my own place and owned two cars, a Mercedes Benz, and a Nissan. Since he no longer had his car, I offered to let him buy my Nissan for a low price, but he wanted it for free because we were dating. I have no idea why I allowed myself to stay with this individual.

As usual, I started catching him cheating like I did almost every low-down dirty boyfriend before him. I even noticed him flirting with other men, like some of my other boyfriends did as well. They were all over the place and lost. I was at the time lost as well to allow so much just for the sake of saying I have love, which was toxic and not love at all. After almost a year of dating, he proposed to me, and I got pregnant. However, the baby was not growing. The doctors mentioned I would have a miscarriage any day. I waited, and it happened. When the miscarriage started, the boyfriend at the time mentioned he didn't care and that he was going to work. So, I called my mother, and she and my aunt took me to the emergency room.

I don't know what my mother was going through, but while I was bleeding out, she began to blame me for what was happening and yelled at me in the hospital room. She didn't know how to cope with her emotions, and it became about her. Her unhealed spirit has always put additional trauma on our circumstances, good or bad circumstances. I felt even more traumatized in the middle of the original traumatic ordeal. I bled out too much and had to be rushed to emergency surgery. My mother did not like how this guy treated me, and I was blamed for it.

Weeks later, he wanted to break up with me, and when I asked him why, he said he just did. Although I was used to men having erratic behaviors, I wanted an explanation. He told me to leave, but I kept pressing for him to tell me why. At this point, he immediately went into a fit of rage and attacked me. He even told me that he put something in my drink to make me lose the baby. I kept trying to get away from him while he chased me all over his uncle's place. His uncle was at work and couldn't help the situation. The boyfriend finally got a hold of me, and that's when he did the unthinkable. He put his 6'4" approximately 230-pound self on me and placed a thick pillow over my face. I was fighting for my life as I tried not to black out. With my hands semi free, I used my nails and clawed him as hard as I could until he got off of me. I finally got away and ended up running outside barefoot and with my clothes hanging off. He chased me outside and across the street to try to finish me off. Some girls who I call my angels saw what was happening and called me into their home. They then called 911.

When the police arrived, the boyfriend spoke to

them first for a while before they came over to the girls' home to speak to me. He had told them a big lie about what happened. He was marked up from scratches, and since he was light-skinned, the marks were easy to see on him. The police briefly spoke to me and asked if I needed to go to the hospital. I told them yes because my whole body hurt, but I was also shaking and in shock. I had marks on my body, as well, but they were less noticeable because of my complexion and melanin in my skin.

The police got into the ambulance with me, and we headed to the hospital. I didn't really think of why the police were riding in the ambulance with me. I was in a state of shock and couldn't think straight. When we arrived at the hospital, the police immediately handcuffed me and told me that I was under arrest. Oh my God! I felt like I was in a twilight zone. I could not believe what was happening. The boyfriend tried to smother and delete me, but I was the one being arrested. I tried pleading with the officers that he had tried doing what I just mentioned. The doctor then came and tried to x-ray me to check for internal injuries, but the police would not remove the handcuffs from my wrists for her to do so. She pleaded with them until they finally allowed her to help me. I was detained at the hospital with the police officers for hours while other cops did a further investigation at the original site of violence. Finally, by night, some police officers came into the hospital and said I was "not under arrest". They mentioned that a few neighbors had witnessed the boyfriend chasing me like a sociopath. My family also called my cop friends to get advice when I was at the hospital, and the cops at the site found out I worked on the Sheriff's Advisory Council, was a community leader, and so on. My life was saved that day by witnesses coming forth, and I never had received a wrongful record of any kind! I thank God so much for saving my life that day and my name. My father went to the scene and saw the boyfriend take off in my car in which I helped him to have, like nothing happened. I believe I looked guilty at first because of my darker skin and also that the crime incident happened at a cop's house as well. There was a thorough investigation, and the police did the rightful thing that day after their mistake was made.

The boyfriend came to my home a few weeks later to the window apologizing. I never answered, and I never heard from him again. Thank God! I was refined in this part of my life and covered by my God to be alive and keep my good name and record. I didn't understand why a person would have so much rage towards someone who was easygoing, a fun person, and had helped him so much. Later, some of his family members told me that he was born with drugs in his system. I had an issue with trying to help people when I saw something off with them. I didn't know when I was younger to run fast from anyone who seemed toxic and especially sociopathic. At this time, I still had a sense of brokenness and needed much healing for myself. I could've avoided these situations, but I didn't have a keen sense of awareness at the time. I felt when things were not right, but I ignored my intuition at the time and wanted to see life and people as potential and what they and we can be and not what it really was. This has been a grand learning experience.

I eventually had to go to the City Attorney's office and have a hearing about the incident. I was advised to leave men alone and focus on continuing my education. I told the courts that I would take their advice, stay to myself and not give attention to any guys for a while. I was back in college and had much success behind me and in front of me; I just wasn't successful in relationships. I was now turning thirty (30), and my life seemed to blossom once I focused on myself.

After my life was saved, I focused hard on my education. I finally graduated from not one, but two community colleges and was in a prep program at the University of California Los Angeles (UCLA) called UCLA's Center for Community Colleges Partnerships. This program would be the turning point of my life which would eventually help me go through the steps to have a fantastic application to apply to one of the top universities in the world, UCLA. I worked so hard during the day and pulled all-nighters. I worked on my college work on Thanksgiving and Christmas breaks and other holidays. I would work on papers, studying and sometimes just catching up on my extensions for my papers. I worked harder once I made up my mind that I wanted to be at UCLA. A counselor at West Los Angeles college told me I didn't have what it took to be at a top world class university like UCLA. I was an honor student all my life and had been very well accomplished and awarded. At the same time, my GPA dropped in community college because in the past, I would start and stop, not being totally committed. Once I took it seriously, like what I do with most things, I knew I would "Succeed"! The counselor didn't know this about me. She just assumed I wouldn't or couldn't do it. I cried after my meeting with her and then brushed myself off, spoke to a motivating friend, and hit the ground running. I had to prove to myself that I could do it, no matter what someone who didn't know me thought. I've had people tell me I wasn't cut out for something, only for me to prove them wrong! This is something you as a reader can incorporate in your life, as well. Don't listen to those naysayers; it doesn't matter who they are. If you believe in something and work hard for it, you can do it! You and the Creator know what has been placed in your heart and God gives us the strength to accomplish it! My twenties were about hurt and pain, but I was well accomplished at that time, as well. The time going into my thirties became about my education and finding my true purpose.

This part of my story is putting me in an emotional state right now, because as I was getting closer to getting into UCLA, my dream school, with so many more opportunities opening up to me and my life starting to feel peaceful, there was a turn during all of this. Now my father all of sudden didn't seem well. Before this happened, there was a man who followed me through

CVS Pharmacy. He followed me down every aisle, but I was so used to men following me and hitting on me, so it wasn't a surprise. When we were at the register, he acted shy and asked if he could give me his card, which showed he was an owner of a Juice It Up franchise. I thought he was nice other than following me, but as I mentioned, I thought it was normal since it happened often with me. We exchanged numbers, and I headed to prepare to stay at UCLA for a summer program for prep work to hopefully be accepted into the university. The guy I met in the store called me on the phone here and there, but I was too busy to speak. Finally, weeks later when I returned home, I was bored and asked if he wanted to finally go out. We ended up going to see live music, and I had to go to rehearsal to perform the Michael Jackson thriller dance at a Beverly Hills MJ tribute due to him recently passing away. I asked the guy if he wanted to come, but he said he couldn't. I ended up going on a few more dates with him, and I felt a little comfortable with him. He seemed quiet and sweet. I told him that I had been through some bad relationships, and I did not want to see anyone. He started pushing the issue that he really wanted to be in a relationship with me. After just a month of going out with him, he bought me a new computer. I kept telling him no and that I had to stay focused, but we could go out here and there. We continued to see each other, and next thing I knew, I was in a relationship with him. I kept thinking about being at the City Attorney's office when the court mediators told me to stay focused and not be bothered by men for a while. It had been about a year since the situation occurred with the previous boyfriend. I felt maybe if I moved slowly, everything would be okay. He seemed different from the others. He was about twelve plus years my senior. He was already in his forties and seemed like a giving person, which was different for me. Guys had always wanted me to give to them because they saw my ambition, drive, success, etc. He seemed to love entrepreneurship, traveling, and started going to church with me. This is something I was always able to get men to do. Men loved following me to church. I thought they wanted to get closer to God, but many of them wanted to see what I was doing and be a part of everything I was a part of and had alternative motives. Anyways, we were dating, and my parents liked him. We were always together, but I kept my focus on UCLA. He seemed to support what I was doing, and he seemed to care about me and me to him.

Now back to the story about my dad. My father and mother liked the fact that I seemed happy now and there were no complaints about my dating thus far. Now, noticing my dad was not well after my life seemed to come together was shocking. My father and I were just starting to have an even closer father/daughter relationship. We communicated more; we spent more time with one another. The older I got, my relationship with him blossomed. I would talk to him daily and nightly. He would call me at night to see if my doors were locked, and we would have middle of the night talks about life. We loved music, so I would call him from concerts, especially of his favorite old school artists. We would also listen to music together, and I would perform, sing, and dance. He would look so proud of me. He would support me at my shows as well and bring me flowers. I was so happy to be close to my dad. I would go by his house to spend time, to check in on him, and we'd just talk and hang out. He was dating a woman who moved into his home with him. They would stay together for about eight years. She seemed to be a nice person. She was an entrepreneur who sold jewelry and clothing at venues. I knew many prominent people and how to build great relationships with people, other than men who chased me with alternative motives. Some of the people I knew were well-known promoters of major celebrity concerts. The promoters liked me, so I would invite people with me to go to concerts and hang out VIP with celebrities. My dad's girlfriend wanted to use my connections to get into these concerts to sell her supplies. Because I wanted my dad happy, and my dad wanted to be in the concert environments, I connected his girlfriend to a promoter who allowed her into many concerts throughout Southern and Northern California and other surrounding cities. My dad was happy, and that is what mattered. I have always loved helping people. I never ask for anything back in return. My heart just feels good to make others happy, and God has always blessed me so I like to give back and I don't ask for things in return for helping them. My father's girlfriend and I seemed to be friends, and she was shocked that my sisters and I accepted her when my dad started dating her. We wanted to see our dad and everyone in a peaceful relationship. What I didn't know was out of the eight years she dated my dad, she actually was using him and using me for her business. I found this out the hard way when my dad started getting ill. Just being too open and trusting of others is what has been my downfall, and I used to stay too long around them after seeing red flags. It took a while to know what red flags even were. This is what I'm teaching others now and why I'm writing this book.

For almost a year, she left my dad. We found out she had another man and was still married to a different man. She left my dad knowing he was getting ill, but my dad and no one was telling his daughters he was ill. I saw my dad when I wasn't busy and just thought he was losing weight due to being healthier since that is what he mentioned. I'm crying now because I did not realize it was unhealthy weight loss and his girlfriend left him like that on purpose. We found that she wanted him gone so she could obtain his house and money. This was stone-cold evil! I kept insisting on my dad going to the hospital because we all knew by this point that he was ill, but he did not want to go. He was afraid of what they would tell him. He didn't tell me that he was throwing up blood, and it was now getting hard for him to sit and stand. I saw my dad start to deteriorate before my eyes and called my sisters to try to come and convince him to go to the hospital. His girlfriend finally appeared back into his life when she found we were trying to help him and that he was deteriorating. At this time, she also had her daughters all about the same ages as me and my sisters who were living in my dad's back house. My sisters and I were not allowed to move in my dad's back house when we needed a place to stay per his girlfriend, but she convinced him to allow her whole family to live in the back house including her mother, her daughters, her daughter's boyfriend, that we know of. They were also her spies. They seemed to be our friends before, but come to find out, they were helping their mom try to get my father's assets. My father's girlfriend didn't even care about my dad. She used him, and I later found out she was a female narcissist after my study on narcissists and narcissistic personality disorder.

I finally got my dad to the hospital. I stayed with him and didn't leave his side as it took a day or so to run tests. His girlfriend did not want to be at the hospital to comfort him, she seemed irritated and made the situation about her. It was urgent for her to start her plan and scheme to organize taking my dad's assets. Eventually, the doctor told my sisters and I that our dad had esophageal cancer and only had two months to live. The cancer had spread throughout his body. This was one of the most devastating days of our lives. My sisters and I were shocked. We screamed and cried throughout the hospital floor.

My sister, Venus, started going through more narcissistic abuse from her husband, who didn't want her to be with our dad while he was suffering. Then my other sister, Jessica, ended up in a very similar situation in her relationship at the time. It was a crazy time with so much going on in one's lives while at the same time watching our dad deteriorate quickly before our eyes.

The final few weeks of my dad's life, he was afraid to go to sleep. So, my sisters and I wanted to be with him in person to comfort him and stay on the phone all night if that's what he needed as well. My father's girlfriend did not want us to talk to him or come by. This was beyond odd. She started becoming a different person. Actually, the mask she had on for so long had completely slipped off. She was now the wicked witch of the east, west, and more. We could not reach our dad on the phone. She isolated him from us while he was passing away. We went looking for him at his home and couldn't get in. His girlfriend and her daughters started arguments with us to leave our dad alone with them while putting together illegal paperwork to obtain my father's assets. We were the next of kin and his girlfriend was still legally married to another man.

The other reasons his girlfriend did not want us to be with him is because at this point, he was in a wheelchair, and she wheeled him all over the city to start putting things in his name for her, including a new van as well. She put together a Living Will, even though my father was not in his right mind due to the cancer spreading to his brain, and she had a notary public go to my dad's house to notarize these documents. She was illegally doing these things while he was dying, and she absolutely did not want us around at all. We fought to see him, and one day, I told her angrily to let us be with our dad. Her daughter wanted to fight me and made it seem like I was the bad person and she gaslighted us to say something was wrong with us because my sisters and I wanted to comfort our dad. My dad's girlfriend manipulated all the parties, telling lies that my dad did not want to see me and vice versa. I was her big threat in ceasing the illegal processes she was doing. I was shocked and got tired of fighting, so I shut down and missed seeing and talking to my dad for the last weeks of his dying. I was in a state of shock, and I couldn't fight any longer. I usually never give up, but this was the time I went into a standstill because the pain was too unbearable. I couldn't even comprehend this type of evil. I really didn't know why this was happening.

Eventually, my dad's siblings, who never truly tried to be kind or have a relationship with us or him, went to my dad's house while he was in hospice, and his siblings told me that he wanted to see me. When I went to see him, he was almost gone. His girlfriend was finished with her illegal paperwork on my father, so it was ok for me to see him at that point. His girlfriend had smear campaigned my sisters and I to my dad's sisters. They went with the smear campaign and started treating my sisters and I badly during my father's passing. They seemed to have no empathy. They even planned his funeral in front of him as he laid there dying. Who does this? This was a true nightmare.

I was expecting everyone to strengthen one another and pray together. Instead, it was a bunch of mess and chaos and hatred. That's when I noticed these people who I really didn't know but shared the same bloodline did not seem to be very good people. Some of them even wanted some of my dad's assets and were easily manipulated by his narcissistic girlfriend. His girlfriend also never wanted us to take my dad to the Veterans Hospital where they were going to give him better care than Kaiser or the lack of care with him under her in hospice. She didn't care anything about him. She also mentioned not having a nurse come to help him in hospice to turn his body and make him comfortable. She opted out of these things and blocked all decisions my sisters and I tried to make for better care for our dad. Finally, in the last week of his life, my sisters and I, along with my mom's sister were able to get my dad to the Veterans Hospital away from the abuse he was going through in hospice with his demonic girlfriend. The doctor at the VA hospital cried when he saw my dad, saying he had never seen bed sores that bad on a patient. My dad was in so much pain while dying, and his girlfriend allowed the pain on purpose. His girlfriend couldn't wait for him to decease so she could finalize the remainder of his assets. She had wiped out his bank accounts and all. My dad had always saved money. My sisters and I were the next of kin, and we were in her way in her eyes. I have always wondered if her daughters ever thought about how they would feel if someone did to them with their father what they did to us with their mother while our father was passing away. He was abandoned and abused in his final days! I can't stop crying as I'm writing and reliving this in my being.

I felt like I was drifting. The suffering was already

tremendous, but she made it a hundred times worse. My dad passed at the Veterans Hospital when my sisters and I were there. During that night, his girlfriend walked in with my dad's sister. They both had such an evil look on their faces, and his girlfriend had a demonic smirk on her face and chewing gum when she came in. It was like something out of a horror movie. That's when I realized more of the demonic evil of the world, and she is a representation of that. Hopefully, she has truly asked God, his true son Jesus Christ into her life and heart since those days.

After my dad passed, his girlfriend wanted control of his body, but my sisters and I took control. Since we were the next of kin, we prepared his funeral and burial arrangements. She and his siblings thought they would do that, and they mocked us by saying we wouldn't even ride in the limo with them and could just bring some food. These people seemed so out of touch with being human. They had no love, no heart. My sisters and I never even received any of our dad's belongings. We were so traumatized and exhausted we never even got the police involved to escort us to get his belongings. I wanted to have some historical belongings to show my children from their grandfather. My dad wanted me to have his high school jacket, and I only wanted his musical records that he had been collecting since he was a little boy, along with his record player and all the pictures of us to show my children and the cards and treasures I gave him on every birthday and Father's Day. His girlfriend sent me and my sisters a $2-dollar bill since my dad also collected those. This was done on purpose to mock us. What evil people do to others eventually comes back on them. God will avenge his people. God, you have strengthened us since that time. I thank You for your strength!

I refined myself after this chapter in my life. I have forgiven my dad's family, but I can no longer associate with people like this who are hurt people hurting others. I'm learning to forgive my dad's girlfriend and her family and God is helping me to do so. I will not forget what they have done, but this has refined me into a much stronger beautiful person. I am forgiving, so God will keep my heart pure and of love. This situation has taught me more about the evil within people and allowing the dark world to use them. I pray they will all truly get to know God, and I know that God has promised to avenge his people. I don't worry because I know God saw everything that happened. I pray that God will also help me to continue to help me get closer to Him to know more of Him through His Word and the Refinement of my Being! If you have experienced hurt like this, just know God witnessed it and avenges his people. Get strong and refine yourself to watch and pray—to not be surprised by evil, but be aware. I pray my dad is with our heavenly Father and the Son of God, Jesus, in heaven and that I and we will see him again in pure happiness in God's Glory.

Reflection: Think of a time when you experienced life-altering hurt. How did you stay strong? What are some of the things you need to heal from and release? Are there any people you need to forgive or work on forgiving? Write your answers, the names of those people, and whatever comes to your mind pertaining to this topic. Pray over this and ask God to strengthen and refine you after the pain and hurt.

Star K. Edwards

_____

_____

_____

_____

_____

_____

_____

_____

_____

_____

_____

_____

_____

_____

_____

_____

_____

Star K. Edwards

_____

_____

_____

_____

_____

_____

_____

_____

_____

_____

_____

_____

_____

_____

_____

_____

_____

Chapter V:

Refining Narcissistic Abuse and the Future Faking of Narcissism

Finally, I was accepted to my dream school, UCLA, to complete my bachelor's and eventually earn my master's degree, which had been a dream of mine. I worked so hard to get into UCLA. When I first applied, I was denied. I worked twice as hard the following year on my work, and finally, UCLA accepted me. This was one of the proudest and happiest days of my life. This university gets over 100,000 applicants every year from around the world. UCLA choses the cream of the crop worldwide to attend this university, and I was one of the ones they had chosen. At this place, I fell more in love with socio-cultural anthropology with my combined love for the arts. Here, I realized I'm supposed to tell stories in inspiring people's lives for the better, including starting with my story and continuing with others. I started to become a sociocultural anthropologist working in media. Sociocultural anthropologists explore how people variously positioned within the world today live and understand the world, their aspirations and struggles, and how shared systems of ideas (i.e., culture) relate to the structured ways that people act and interact in society (i.e., power etc.). I was able to come up with the idea to use the study of human beings and learn their stories then bring awareness to their stories through media. Also, to show how we are interrelated in many ways. Also, mostly to show we are spiritual beings having a human experience.

Before getting accepted into UCLA, while attending West LA college and while my father was living, I had panic attacks so bad that it was hard to walk out of the house. It was hard to drive, but I found a college bus that took me to West LA College. I would leave my car parked and take the metro bus to the college bus, refusing to let my panic attacks stop me from living my dreams of attending UCLA and making a great mark on society! I had panic attacks in classes, but I pushed through. I wasn't going to let anything stop my success. I eventually achieved one of my greatest accomplishments even though the counselor at West LA College said I wouldn't. Good thing I never listened to the naysayers. Before my father passed away, he also told me that I would do it, and I did!

While grieving my dad's death, I had to strengthen myself to start this very challenging university. I was glad I had much experience and accomplishments. Now I just needed the degrees, and then I would have experience *and* education, which equals remarkable success. This education also helped me focus more on my purpose and opened the door to many unbelievable opportunities. One thing I should have done at the time was leave the relationship I was in. I continued my relationship with the boyfriend I met at CVS, but he did not fit well into my plans for success. He had a stable job, but I eventually learned he didn't want much or couldn't dream big like me. I believe this was a cultural issue as well. Later, I also found out that he just mirrored the things I liked so I would think I found someone who would be good in my life. My idea about what he wanted in life was the opposite and far from what I thought; I wanted him to be something he was not. I would eventually find out we were not compatible. Not only that, but he was someone who did not have good intentions.

One of the issues in relationships is having sex with someone before knowing if the two of you are compatible. Also, having sex before marriage. Sex ties your soul to people you may not have anything in common with other than sex. This is what happened to me.

I'm the type of person who is called an empath. An empath is highly attuned to other people's emotional experiences. If you can tap into the feelings of those around you, you more than likely are able to better support and care for people. Empaths are giving, nurturing, and caring. We have good intuitions, but the downside of being an empath is ignoring our intuition at times due to wanting to see the good in people and situations, even when they are not good. We give people many chances after hurting us. We make the mistake of thinking if we love someone hard enough, they will respond to our love with love, and everything will be fine. This is usually not the case. This is a part of ignoring our intuition and not wanting to think someone can be as bad as what they are showing us. If we were to listen to our intuition, we would see people and situations for what they actually are and not what we think they should be.

Well, that's what I did in this relationship. I thought I learned my lesson from the previous relationship, which I mentioned in the previous chapter, but I had not truly learned. I had to go through some of these things to become the person I am today. I had to also go through the refinement process to grow closer to wholeness and have this story to tell that will help others.

My relationship started off well. He seemed to even be there for me when my dad passed away. He loaned me money for my father's funeral including the funds I received out of my 401K plan when family members or my dad's girlfriend did not put any funds on the funeral. This was nice of him, other than some of the good qualities he had, there were red flags in the relationship from the beginning, but I ignored them. Due to having been around toxicity while growing up, I didn't realize what red flags even were. Before I speak further about this relationship, I want my readers to know again that I had a pattern of being in relationships with toxic men. The world is a fallen place, and there are a lot of toxic people amongst us in the midst of good people. Due to my warm personality, I gravitated at times to people with motives. Unfortunately, the bad ones were more aggressive and manipulative in getting into my life than good people. I now see right through them after going through these major refinement processes.

When I started this relationship, he love-bombed me so hard. Love bombing is lavishing the utmost attention, adoration, affection, etc., in order to influence or manipulate a person. This is toxic because it makes the person who is on the receiving end struggle in maintaining personal boundaries at times.

After being duped into feeling like we may be in love, he started devaluing me. Devalue is to reduce or underestimate the worth or importance of, to tear down, or break apart. Everything seemed beautiful in the relationship, but then things happened. I was still seeking the love I thought he had for me. The height of the devaluing phase came once my father passed away, we got married and after the birth of our first child. Before things took a turn, we were spending a lot of time with one another. We went to church together every Sunday for four years. I seemed to have found the best man, or so I thought. Not too many men who I came across were single, mature, good men. So, I fell for this one, thinking I could work with him and he could work with me. It seems to not be much to choose from, so I went for what I thought could be workable.

We had a lavish wedding up in the beautiful wealthy hills of Rancho Palos Verdes, California. Many people have said that we had the most beautiful wedding they have ever been to, and many said it was because it was my beauty that touched the wedding. I was so happy on that day. He seemed happy, as well, even with tears in his eyes. He had been saying he wanted to marry me from the first month or so of us dating. I found out later that coming on too strong to someone you don't even know and making major plans with basically a stranger is a red flag.

We were married, and after the wedding, we headed to a local island on a boat. He appeared to be so happy and emotional during the ceremony, but after eyes were off of him, he was a bully. I didn't realize I was in an abusive relationship. I didn't understand the crazymaking behavior when things were supposed to be fine. Why would anyone not want peace, love, and happiness? It's beyond my comprehension.

During my pregnancy, the emotional and mental abuse went to another level, and that's when the devaluation went to another level. He now felt like he had me locked in. I did not realize what was really happening, but it seemed all so familiar to me due to other men treating me badly and having a family who devalues. I stayed in the relationship due to those familiar spirits. At the time, I couldn't pinpoint what was wrong with this. All I know is that my internal spirit didn't feel right. Something deep down inside felt broken, and the abuse made me feel even more broken, especially when it came to being with child and going through what seemed like the height of abuse. Still, I tried so very hard to make the marriage work.

After we were married, I moved into the UCLA family housing, which was a beautiful housing village for UCLA affiliates, especially graduate students, professors, scientists, and doctors working their residency etc. The community had many pregnant women and young children. Most people were in their thirties (30s) in University Village, which was the average age professionals started their families. There were also many married people living in this village. The support that was given amongst the people and seeing those same individuals at our children's daycare center, on the UCLA campus, and at home in our village made it feel like a military base and a great community of people from all over the world. I loved living there! I made friends from all over the world who are now world scientists, including myself as a social scientist.

Going back to my story, after my new husband signed the move-in contract, he was given access to the village. Around this time, I was preparing to have my firstborn son. I thought my husband was moving in as well since he had signed the lease with me. We were newly married and needed a home for us to start our family. This is what I thought, but this is not what was in his head. He had alternative motives. Everything we discussed was not what he had in mind, and he wouldn't tell me his motives and intentions, which I later found out were cruel intentions. Months had gone by, and I kept asking him when was he going to move into our place at University Village. He kept starting unnecessary arguments and gaslighting me with crazy making conversations. Gaslighting is to manipulate someone by psychological means into questioning their own sanity. This went on for months, and I started hearing from him less. It got to the point where he wouldn't return my phone calls and would block me from calling.

I eventually gave birth to our first son, which was the most beautiful day of my life other than giving birth to our other son. My husband at the time was there during the process with my mother and sister. After they left, and I was in post birth care, he treated me so badly during my hospital stay after giving birth. The staff who helped me with my birth were so pleasant and caring. I thank God for that. My husband did try to help me with the baby at times, but his energy and attitude were off. He even told me rather harshly to quiet the baby so he could get some sleep, and this was just a few hours after giving birth. I kept noticing something was off with this guy, but as I mentioned, I was used to the familiar spirits of people around me for many years of my life.

After going home from the hospital, I remember having him and my mother there. Both devalued everything I did and yelled at me. It was horrible. I took care of my baby so well, but they both seemed not to want to be there to help. My mother and husband eventually left, and I finally had peace with my baby. It was hard to take care of my baby alone, but it was better than getting emotionally and mentally abused every second and walking on eggshells. I was waiting to have love and support shown, but it never came. I was shown the lack of these things most of my life by toxic people. Outside people have mostly treated me with adoration and respect.

While getting used to being a new mom, I eventually realized my husband was not moving in with me. He had no intention of moving in. He and his mother planned for him to remain living with her, and they never told me, just gaslit me into feeling like I was doing something wrong, instead of openly explaining the position. He had married me, and we made plans—or I should say he pretended to make plans with me, but he never told me the truth that he never intended on living like he was married. I had never heard of anything like this before in my life—a person getting married but never telling the other person that they are not moving in and leaving them to figure it out on their own.

One of the games he also played was attending church with me every Sunday for four years and then saying he did not have to go to church anymore after marrying me. Going to church with me all that time was also planned out. I thought it was to get closer to God and build a relationship with our Heavenly Father. This was not the thinking he had; it was about him and getting me under his control, but I did not realize this at the time.

He played a lot of mind games with me, and it increased after the wedding and after I became a mom. He wanted people to see him get married to an incredible person for his image and to hide things he was doing. I was a cover up for him and did not realize it. I eventually realized that everything was a game to him; my life was a game to him. He played with my life and kept telling me to just get over it. I was just trying to live happily, peacefully, and have a family, but he imitated what I wanted, and his mask eventually started slipping off. He was someone I didn't know. He promised me a marriage that I never had and to be a father for our children. He set up future faking for me. I am glad that he is now being a father.

What is future faking? Future faking is a manipulative tactic designed for coercion, control, and distraction. Narcissists use future faking to mimic the life their victim envisions and the goals their victim sets. What is a narcissist? It's not what many people think of as the person in the mirror all day. The term narcissist is deeper than that. It is a term combined with narcissistic personality disorder, which is one of several types of personality disorders where people have an inflated sense of their own importance and a deep admiration for themselves. They have very troubled relationships and lack empathy for others. These people get into relationships to manipulate and control a person, and they are very abusive. They lie, cheat, gaslight, and more. They ruin lives, and what's troubling is that they are hard to spot until you are already deep in a relationship with them and have invested so much. The person I married used daily bullying and gaslighting, especially after he had me all the way invested. Then the mask slipped off.

I was also going through postpartum depression, which can sometimes result from not having support or experiencing major life stressors after giving birth. I still didn't know why he wasn't living with me at the time. He came around some, and I thought we were working on our marriage. Then surprise! I got pregnant with our second son. This was a shocker. I was more fertile than I thought. I had just finished nursing my firstborn, and I guess the birth control method I used failed to do its job. I didn't think this would happen, but it did. My son and both son(s) were meant to be here.

During the time of my second pregnancy was the height of narcissistic abuse. I found sex workers information, and then there was another woman I found about who he was seeing in Brazil while we were together. I found so many things that I can't even name them all. He was living a double life. That's one reason he wanted to live with his mother instead of the person he married. He was an old bachelor and just "future faked" it all with me. I was in my deepest depression ever while pregnant with my second son due to what I was experiencing. I will mention more about narcissistic abuse in one of my next books.

I eventually gave birth and had to stay in the hospital for some days from some complications, but we made it through! After I gave birth to my second son, I was then ghosted for a little while by the person I married. He stopped answering my calls because he was living another life and like some men who never grew up, they don't want to be responsible, but live a life of fun. The crazy thing about this situation is his mother was co-signing everything he was doing. I couldn't imagine another woman not having empathy for her grandchildren and her daughter-in-law. I would call her crying, but his mother didn't care. I eventually found out she was the matriarch head narcissist. It was devastating to find out that they both faked everything with me and partnered together for him to try to destroy me and for him to not be responsible at the time. I started reacting to his abuse, which is called reactive abuse. It put my body in a state of shock and beyond heightened anxiety. At this point, I found out how evil people are in the world.

His mother had a very large picture in her living room showing that she was an ordained minister. It's crazy how many people play with God and have people fooled so they can manipulate and abuse others. What was even more of an eye-opener is that I always thought mostly men contributed to messing up children's lives. It was devastating to find out it's many toxic and evil mothers who do this.

His mother started intentionally falling out of the bed when he would come see me and spend time with our baby boys. She would try to hurt herself and have to go to the hospital because her son, who in her mind was supposed to be like her husband, would leave her for a couple of hours to be with his children and me, who was his wife. She would call his phone back-to-back to get him to come back home to her. This was a very toxic mother-son relationship. I didn't notice how codependent and beyond sickening it was until he was married to me and had children. This grown man never wanted to leave his mother, but he wanted to trap me. He knew I would need him once I had his children, and that way, he could have full control over me. This was some beyond sickening and devilish plan.

I can't go into too much detail until my next book, but I wanted to provide you with a tiny snippet of what I went through in a narcissistic abusive relationship or as survivors call it, a situationship. He almost destroyed me. I found out what I was dealing with by googling abuse one day while pregnant with my second son, and narcissistic abuse started being revealed after I started researching the behaviors of what I identified. That's when God answered my prayers on what this was and then led me to YouTube videos. I finally had answers for the behavior of the person and my experiences, which were not of this world. I finally started getting answers about my childhood and how a person's programming from their parents determines how we see ourselves and what we will allow in relationships. I had no boundaries. I had to refine myself and learn to have boundaries and stop trying to overly please people to think they will behave and treat me well. YouTubers helped me with this. Many of them experienced the things I have written about in this book. The first YouTuber I started listening to pertaining to this was Dana Morningstar's *Thrive After Abuse*. This was an eye-opener and literally saved my life.

When my sons grow up and ask me what happened during this time, I will tell them that a person can change if they want, but no one or nothing will make them. We have free will to be good or bad in this life and suffer the consequences during life and after death. They will know that the very person who hurt me and is a part of them has an opportunity to change if he opens his heart up to God and allows Him into his heart and soul. The same goes for the person reading this book. You, too, have to be willing to open yourself up and accept Jesus Christ as your Lord and Savior and if you truly do, others will see your light and witness the fruits you bear by loving Him and one another, no matter the individual.

I have eventually forgiven him for what he's done. I won't forget, but I had to forgive so I can continue to allow God to use me in my life. He is now a consistent father and shows support and care for our boys continuously. We are learning to be co-parents, and he has calmed down due to me not asking him to be responsible. He is doing it now on his own. He is there for our sons without any pressure from me. I pray that God will continue to touch him and that my sons' father will continue to be there for our boys. I've learned my lesson, and I won't have bitterness in my heart. I had to learn to forgive him and others so I can be free in my being. I will keep my heart pure, and you can do the same as a reader of this book. You'll see how in my story.

Reflection: Think of a time when or if someone told you a life-altering lie. How did you stay strong? What are some of the things you need to heal from and release? Are there any people you need to forgive or work on forgiving? Write your answers and the names of the people. Pray over it, and ask God to strengthen and refine you after the pain and hurt. Write whatever comes to your mind pertaining to this topic.

Star K. Edwards

_____

_____

_____

_____

_____

_____

_____

_____

_____

_____

_____

_____

_____

_____

_____

_____

_____

_____

Star K. Edwards

_____

_____

_____

_____

_____

_____

_____

_____

_____

_____

_____

_____

_____

_____

_____

_____

Chapter VI:

Refining Church Hurt. Oh My!

The crazymaking and narcissistic abuse in my so-called fake marriage led me to reach out to people. Not in my right self, I even went on social media one day and reached out for help. My family was going through their own situations and trying to heal. Regarding friends, I was transitioning at the time, seeing which ones were loyal friends, but they were busy and going through their life situations, too. I eventually turned to my church and a new small group I started attending, hoping someone would hear me out. I understood my life problems shouldn't become other people's problems. At the same time, if people are in church every Sunday learning the word of God, then they should be familiar with a verse that says to bear one another's burdens. I didn't want to burden anyone, but I was literally losing it!

Running to people at church was the worst thing I could have done. Some people in church can be more unloving and unforgiving than the people in the world who don't attend church. It seems backwards. Many churches are just an organization to look powerful, have people be noticed, have social gatherings, and be a place for entertainment. This is not what God wants. Some people think church is a place to look as if you have it going on, pretend to have everything together, and mock and look down on others who are going through life struggles. The church I was attending seemed to have some people like that there. I tried looking for another church, but they all have good and bad mixed within. People not showing love within the church has changed what God originally designed. All I want to do is get together with people who have love in their hearts, show empathy, and have the Holy Spirit. If an increased number of people instruct this, then there would be an outpouring of love and empathy coming from people and an outpouring of the Holy Spirit. But at times, it's not. Also, church is a breathing ground for some narcissists. They target churches, and some of them are in leadership roles. They want to be recognized, looked up to, and pretend as if they know God. It's an illusion. I've met too many of these types of people and can pinpoint them now because God has opened up my intuition. I've transitioned to the next stage in my life, which is an awakening, and I thank God for it. The old me is gone! It has shed away.

One example of church hurt I've experienced was when going through the height of narcissistic abuse and other major life circumstances, I was also a new mother with two babies. People looked down on me because they didn't see a husband with me and knew I was going through some trauma within my marriage. Non loving people in the church did not try to see that I was a well-accomplished person like many of them or most importantly, a child of God. I even tried to show them I am one of His. I sought community because I did not want to lose it especially while being a new mother. I wanted to gain my strength but needed a sense of love, support, and community within the church.

My church had been considered a multicultural third culture evangelical covenant church. I felt I had a connection there with many of us having attended the same universities, UCLA, USC, etc., even though our connection should be because we are children of God and followers of Christ. One thing many people in this church had in common was most were married. My sister and I recently called some churches The Happy Marriage Organization, based on our experience. Some women seem to be ostracized if they are not married or divorced with children, etc. within churches.

As I mentioned, to be accepted in some Christian churches, you must look like your life is put together and have the perfect image. Many of the churches these days have lost and don't have the power of the Holy Spirit. A large number of them are about how much money they will make and not about helping people to restore their lives, helping people to gain the strength and power to walk with Christ daily with the Holy Spirit guiding, and they are at times not focused on helping people's souls be saved for Christ Jesus, which is supposed to be the center focus of the church. As I mentioned as well, I've noticed that some churches look down on women who are divorced or single parents. In some of their eyes, what type of asset are you with this on your plate? People within the church are not supposed to be or think this way. This is not how the Lord sees us. People in the church are still people and some may know how to quote scriptures, have leadership positions, and even preach the Word very well, but that doesn't mean they really know Christ Jesus or have truly accepted Him. The enemy of God even knows the Word very well. Some come into the church for alternative motives and to look the part of a Godly person and want to feel powerful, a sense of control and have others follow them, instead of following Christ Jesus. There are also people of God within churches who are there to do the right thing and to be there for the right reasons. We just have to have discernment on where God needs us to be to gain strength with others in growing close to Him. At this particular time in my life, I decided to join a small family group in my church with my two babies so I could be around people and not be home alone. I felt it would also help me get out of my deep depression. I started going to a small group leader's house at my church, which was for families who were married and had children. I was technically still married but didn't know if my marriage would be restored. At the time, I didn't know I was dealing with someone narcissistic.

The married couple who hosted the small group was a white Jew and an Asian. They seemed very unwelcoming when I came to their house. The first time I went to their home for a bible small group gathering, my two babies were with me. When I stepped into their home, I wasn't thinking and went into the living room area with my shoes on. The husband yelled at me, "You don't know when you go into an Asian person's house, you're supposed to take off your shoes!" I was thinking to myself, of course, I know this. I've traveled the world, studied cultures, and have a gift of connecting with people and cross-culturally. I was well-educated, but he treated me like I wasn't. I was just being a mom, paying attention to my children, and forgot to remove my shoes. I didn't mean to disrespect their home.

We would have bible study and deep discussions in their home. One of the things I brought up to the husband was I wanted to know his opinion on a new topic in which Black people may have a different background than what has been taught. I was starting to hear this information, and some studies showed this, even in the bible, many of the people are really supposed to be of color. I sincerely did not want to offend anyone but wanted to get his opinion. I didn't know for sure; I just knew many people were starting to talk about this topic.

As took my babies to their house two Sundays a

month, and even though the couple would see me struggling with my babies, they would not help me. They always had a look of disgust on their face towards me. I believe it was because I overshared information about abuse in my marriage, which I later learned was narcissistic abuse. This is a whole other level of abuse, which includes addictions, cheating, smear campaigning, mind manipulation, trying to destroy a person intentionally, etc. Imagine going through all of that and having two little ones to take care of.

There was another married couple in the small group who also decided to become leaders in the church. I would run into them at church, but the wife stopped speaking to me for whatever reason, and her husband would give me weird looks. I would see the small group leader at the YMCA, and she would not say hello, even when it was just the two of us in the bathroom. I know I overshared in our small group, but I needed someone. Yet, this small group was unloving and didn't want to hear what I was going through. I didn't realize I was becoming a burden. Overall, these people didn't display the love of God. On my part, I wish I had never gone through what I went through in my life. Then I wouldn't have had to trouble other people who didn't care anything about me and didn't see me as a sister in Christ. They acted as if I was not a part of them. I found out later that I wasn't because I had and have the love of God within my heart and walk with his spirit daily.

Because of the unwelcoming, hateful spirit that people had in this small group, I decided to leave. I'm sure the people were relieved. I was so used to having favor most places I went and people showing love and respect towards me because I give people love and empathy. Toxic, bad-spirited people are usually the ones who don't like me. When good-spirited people love me, they really love me, and when evil and bad-spirited people hate me, they really hate me. It was interesting that within the church, I didn't get the basic love, respect, care, or empathy that I do outside of the church. I was torn in my spirit and now going through much depression because of church hurt. Still, I tried to stay strong for my babies. The small group from church never contacted us after we left to see if we were okay or needed anything, but I noticed they would do this for others. They would act like they were concerned and would support other people.

When we left, there were no calls, nothing. Months later, I contacted the wife of the small group and asked her, "How come no one has reached out to check on my babies and I?" She told me she never reached out because she didn't like me! She was so truthful and bold. This was one of the most devastating days of my life. I cried so hard! I called another pastor who had just left the church and cried while telling him what had happened. This was so unbelievable to me. I would never have done or said this to anyone, especially within a so-called Christ community and to someone who was in a life crisis. I could not believe there was so much hate in a church! They did not care that I had two babies—two years old and a new baby. I told the wife that I thought this was what the group was about as well—supporting people in need and who was going through major life circumstances. Also, for people to have their fellow brothers and sisters in Christ to lean on. I guess this wasn't their plan for everyone. What if they had another person in their presence in need? What if the person was facing a life-or-death situation or was on the verge of suicide? With the hurt added by the church group to whatever else was going on with the person, it could be the last straw. With people like this, they wouldn't even care.

Church hurt is like no other. People believe they are surrounded by good people who have accepted God and the Lord Jesus into their hearts. This was an eye-opener and revelation on church hurt. This made me realize that everyone who sits in church every Sunday doesn't know Christ. They are pretending. You would know by their fruits the ones who really know Christ. These fruits were of the enemy. Even the other couple didn't speak to me any longer because I was going through things at the time. I asked God why these people were so evil, and I heard the voice of God say it was racism. I said, *God, but the pastor is Black*. The pastor at the time was a distinguished Black man. I asked God, if they were racist, why are they going to church with a Black pastor?

The other couple who stopped speaking to me eventually moved to the east coast. They said their goodbyes in front of the church and on a YouTube recording. She mentioned that going to the church made her more tolerant of people of color. This was a confirmation from God of what he told me about the people in that small group being racists. This was the definition of church hurt, but this is something they will have to deal with God. This was one of their tests. We all have life tests to pass to be with God and fully in His Glory.

I eventually looked for another church home, but a mostly Caucasian church seemed to close its doors to us when we tried to get back in one day. Searching for another church was not easy. During the time of the pandemic, I went back to the church, first online where these people treated me badly. I did so because I had met many other good people there and planned to be around those people who showed the love of Christ. I'm also praying for those in church who only pretend to know Him and not show the fruits of knowing him. They showed fake fruits in front of others and seem to want to look powerful and respected in leadership roles.

Before leaving the church and then when I gradually went back, I was blessed to have a prayer team who were good people. Three members came to my home for weeks to have deep prayer, therapy talk, and uncover the deep root of my pain. I want to also mention good people like this who are in churches. I don't want to only focus on the bad, but I want people to know the condition of churches and that it is also a hotspot for narcissists, especially in leadership roles. To my readers, we must not let evil drive us out of the church. We must be the light and continue to shine within and outside the church. We can fellowship with people truly seeking

Star K. Edwards

God, walking in His ways, and demonstrating His love!

Reflection: Have you ever been hurt by people you believed would show you love, the love of God? Have you ever been hurt by anyone in church? How did you stay strong? What are some of the things you need to heal from and release? Are there any people you need to forgive or work on forgiving? I encourage you to still love God and grow closer to Him, no matter what people may do negatively in church. You can fellowship with those who walk with God's spirit and not allow others to do damage. Write your answers and anything else that comes to mind pertaining to the topic. Then pray and ask God to strengthen you and refine your life after the pain and hurt.

Star K. Edwards

Chapter VII:

Refining My New Motherhood— the Happiness and the Struggles

When I gave birth to my two baby boys, I instantly fell into a love like no other kind of love, it's beyond anything you can think of! My heart has been full of love at having given life to my beautiful two little boys. When I first laid eyes on them, they both were and are so special and cute. It has been a miracle to give life. There is no feeling like becoming a mother. I wanted to keep that dream-like feeling, but it was so hard for me to enjoy becoming a new mother because of the narcissistic abuse I endured. This should've been the best time of my life, but it was made exceedingly difficult for me at first. I thought I had done everything right. I got married, had success behind my name, and balanced my success with a new success of having education. Then I waited and prepared for motherhood. I felt like everything had lined up for me. I just let the wrong person have access to my womb.

Women must think hard about who we allow access to our wombs. One of the reasons I'm writing and authoring this book is so others will know when to walk away and not invest one's life (and womb) with a so-called fool. I told my ex-husband that he wasn't just a fool but a stone-cold fool for all he'd done to me, especially while I was becoming a mother. He just smirked, thinking it was cool. It was pure evil. Be aware of the evil people in this world—those who seem normal in public but take their masks off in private with their family, loved ones, and other victims. These were the people who gravitated to my light. The dark comes to destroy the light, but it didn't work with me!

I struggled with having two babies. Imagine going through the things I've mentioned in this book and other stories I haven't revealed. Not to mention suffering from sleep deprivation. I also did not have anyone to help me with my two babies at that time of my life, which are under two years apart. I saw mothers fly in from other countries from the other side of the world to UCLA University Village to help their daughters during the birthing process and after. I felt so much in shock that my immediate family was in the same city, and I didn't get help. This brought me into even more awareness of the toxicity which surrounded my life and why I had fallen into more of it and that there were some major chains needed to be broken. I felt like I was losing it, but God continued to strengthen me. I made sure to always dress up and show up. I had to do this so I would not entirely lose myself and I had to appear happy for my children. People who didn't know me would see me and think I had it all together at times. Mothers of all cultures in my community, especially in the UCLA community, would ask me how I keep it together. They had no idea what I was going through, but I had to pull myself together.

What made motherhood even harder was taking my children to the UCLA daycare preschool in our UCLA community. They were babies and attended this preschool for almost five years. The director was Persian, and her manager was a white Latina who could pass for white. They were considered to not like people of color and tried to run melanated people of color who were UCLA affiliates out of the daycare with our children. We were harassed as we dropped off our children, who ranged in age from newborn to almost five years old. I figured it was a racial situation when I asked other people of color about their experiences, and it was confirmed there were many other complaints of this with them as well. I had not experienced much racism until I dealt with this situation. The daycare teachers who were of color confirmed the same things were happening to them, as well.

I had my second child as a small infant in the daycare; his brother was two years old and my 2nd son started at 5 months old at the daycare while I attended

UCLA. The not so good-spirited Latina teacher in the infant classroom seemed to have a bad attitude when it came to me, but she, the director, and other workers would treat people of European descent so well when they came in. It was like a twilight zone. The beautiful-spirited teachers said they were looking out for my children, and my children seemed happy at the daycare. I prayed constantly that they were protected.

I was getting funding for my children to attend that daycare. I needed this to complete my education at UCLA, so I put it in God's hands and waited to see if I needed to move them. I could have taken them to another place in the affluent West Los Angeles area where we lived, but it could have been a similar situation. The director and her colleague knew I was going through troubles as a mother, especially having seen me cry a couple of times when dropping my babies off at daycare. So, they called me into a meeting with them. That's when I broke down and told them about the narcissistic abuse, how my children's father discarded me and left me a single mother (separated from a husband, a person I married). I did not mention the harassment they were putting me through while dropping my children off so I could go to classes at UCLA and complete my education. So many obstacles were coming at me all at once, yet I continued to push through to succeed.

The director and her manager gaslit me in that meeting to get information out of me so they could contact Children Services. Next thing I knew, child services were at my door. This was another obstacle I faced. The racism to get us out of the daycare was used this way. I was told this also happened to other mothers of color whose children went to that daycare. Racism is set up to destroy people and oppress them. It can also be viewed as spiritual warfare because people of color have something special to where people always want to focus on us. After being harassed by a social worker for weeks, Children Services finally realized I was a great mother and just going through a tough time. A UCLA social worker, the director of students with dependents, the Children Services social worker, and I were called to a meeting. The social worker was told to stop hounding me and allow me to complete my exams at UCLA. Children Services never opened a case. I had much support behind me. People who knew me knew who I was and told them I was an astounding person.

The director and the colleague were trying to destroy me, but it didn't work. From that day on, I walked into the daycare like myself again. I did my hair, put on my makeup, dressed up, held my head high, and did not shed a tear. They seemed shocked that they couldn't break me because my children and I have God on our side! Also, racism at the daycare started getting exposed. We put on a theater show with people who came from Brazil to tell our stories, especially the stories of harassment of people of color in the UCLA community and daycare. They eventually had to have racial bias training, and things seemed to get better.

When the COVID-19 pandemic hit and my children

left the school, the director eventually walked up to me and apologized for any harm she may have caused and for not knowing she was being racist. I hope it was a sincere apology. If it were, that was God touching her heart. If it weren't, that would be on her and her heart. I pray to God and hope it was sincere.

After a few weeks of meeting with the social worker, who represented me in the meeting to help me, she passed away from self-conclusion. She was going through her own struggles. She helped me and others but took her own life weeks later. I cried so hard for her; she was such a beautiful person. I even attended her funeral. I believe the weight of this world and being a part of many people's traumas and stories as well took a toll on her.

About a year or so after this incident, I was at my baby's pediatrician. I was still feeling a little out of it from the continuous crazymaking of narcissistic abuse due to me having to still stay in contact with him due to having children. Plus, I tried to encourage him to help me with our children, but at the time, he manipulated and played with my emotions, gaslighting me whenever I asked him for help. This led me to ask for help in various places.

Still going through some depression and trauma from the narcissistic abusive relationship, I started talking about many things regarding my abuse, not realizing who I was telling. I told the nurse these things during my children's pediatric appointment. The doctor came in, took my oldest son, and left for at least thirty minutes. I sat there waiting for the doctor to bring him back. When I opened the door to look for her, there were about at least four police officers at the door, mad-dogging me, looking at me like I was a criminal. This was a total nightmare. A lady finally came into the room. Without identifying herself, she started asking questions about my motherhood. After our meeting, she said there was nothing wrong with me. She mentioned that I was just an overwhelmed mother going through a lot, then she let me go home with my children.

That was another devastating day of my life. Going through this type of abuse and during the time of being a new mother, led me to keep asking for help and sometimes in the wrong places and situations. I could have sued most of those people if I had the strength back then to do so. I was vulnerable and ended up in an abusive situation, but I am also a fighter and eventually became feisty towards him to let him know I would no longer tolerate his schemes and that I was aware of his tactics. Most of the situations I found myself in with people stemmed from the narcissistic abuse I was enduring, which led to more racism because I started to be viewed as a woman of color going through things. You are not allowed to go through major life situations or have mental breakdowns as a person of color. That is what I learned through all of this. You have to keep it together and advance higher than everyone to avoid being harassed and criminalized.

After leaving the hospital in Redondo Beach, where they sent the police because I was breaking down, I waited for the hospital to call and apologize. I called day after day and left messages, but not one person ever responded to my calls except my children's pediatrician. All she said was that she had never seen me that way before. I believe others in her staff made the call. I eventually found out that race had a lot to do with why they never called to apologize for the additional trauma they put on my children and I on that day. I also heard what was in the report from that day, and it was nothing like what actually happened. I was criminalized for needing help. This was something else I had to get over during my new motherhood.

During all of this, my children had not always been good sleepers. One of my sons, when he was a baby, needed tonsil surgery. He had difficulty breathing and sleeping for the first couple of years of his life, and doctors could not figure out what was wrong. This also led to tremendous stress on me as a mother. I was not getting any sleep, and seeing my baby struggle to breathe was heartbreaking and devastating. On top of the abuse and abandonment, this led me to have breakdowns eventually and in front of people. I didn't need the extra bullying, gaslighting, or mind manipulation. Going through narcissistic abuse will destroy your life, and you become criminalized while being victimized.

When my second son was a newborn, and my first was turning two years old, the person I married was reprimanded by the authorities for threatening me after I went to his job looking for him after he ghosted me and told me to lose his number. He never gave any explanation why after I had just married him and given birth to his two children. If I had not married someone like this, motherhood could have been a peaceful, happy time for me, which I deserved.

All of these life traumas have passed, and I'm able to enjoy my beautiful little boys and what motherhood brings. The hard baby years have come and gone, and I know how to deal with narcissists now as well as show others how to deal with them. Because I'm stronger, the abuse has slowed down tremendously; He is now helping more with his children. I pray he will fully get to know God one day. He didn't have to put us through those things. It was totally unnecessary. I did everything I could to be a good woman and make him happy. I have done everything in my power to fight this fight—fighting the enemy who's been using people in my life. I now know to run at the first sign of toxicity.

I thank God that I can now enjoy motherhood. I wish I had pictures of my pregnancy with me dressed in beautiful flowing gowns and glowing with pure happiness. I can now enjoy what I thought could be, but it is now. I'm so glad I had my University of California Los Angeles (UCLA) family housing community as support during that time, especially my Mormon community friends. I've always been strong and courageous, but this was when I couldn't do it all alone because I was in a vulnerable state being a new mother. Things eventually got better.

During their first year of life, my babies practically

grew up at UCLA. They were with me in classes as I nursed them, holding them to the left while writing with my pen to the right. My firstborn son was with me on a project through UC Berkeley and UC Center Sacramento when he was turning nine months old. We were there alone in northern California for a few weeks as I worked producing stories for the California State Capitol and NBC news station, interviewing California's leaders, including senators and congressmen. I also conducted research at the California Secretary of State's office, retrieving historical information from the archives to produce stories. This was an exciting but also challenging time for me not having support. Whenever I would reach out to my husband via phone, he would gaslight me. There were other times when I couldn't reach him at all.

While I was on my work and educational trip, I was glad that my husband back then flew in on the weekends, using flight benefits, to see our baby. He was distant towards me, but he seemed to enjoy the baby, which was a good thing. This was a time I had the opportunity to advance my career. Thankfully, my infant child was taken care of while I worked on these projects that required me to travel to Northern California. Many people in my circle were new parents who did the same. We found our support systems as we built our careers for our families. I had to continue to work when I became a mother and took advantage of these major opportunities when they came my way. This was part of building a legacy for my children. I took care of my babies first before everything else, and when I needed breaks for me and my boys, I took them and still do. Sometimes I take a couple of days or so to rest, then move forward. I push through and get the work done; people admire that about me.

I have had a lot of good people support me in the midst of my working and being a mother. Because of my hard work, I was accepted into the University of Southern California (USC) to complete one last degree while building my business. I also have started the process to start lecturing at colleges and universities part-time as a sociocultural visual anthropologist while running my visual media company. Also, another fantastic opportunity which came my way before the pandemic was when a United States ambassador who recruits at UCLA asked me to go through a program to become a United States Ambassador. I was offered to live in another country representing the U.S. If I would have accepted the position, my children would have gotten the opportunity to attend private schools in foreign countries and have a paid nanny. I was offered to also work in the media as a U.S. ambassador, where I found that ambassadors work on different projects within their field. This was a grand opportunity and there are other opportunities which have been offered to give my children a grand legacy and life.

I have continuously had favor even in the midst of adversity. I thank God for all the opportunities to build a grand legacy for my children. These opportunities would help our family for life—to work hard now and soon reap the benefits. We have persevered through all of this. I have totally refined myself as a mother and human being. My boys, turning six and eight years old at the time of my writing this book, are growing up to become very cultured, fine, brilliant young men. They will contribute so many remarkable things to our family, their families and society. They have been given a more privileged life because of my hard work, which is providing them with the tools they need to be successful. I'm working hard to give them everything they need spiritually, mentally, emotionally, physically, etc. Also, I thank God for the turnaround from their father, who is doing a good job at co-parenting and for being there for our boys, speaking to them consistently every day, spending time with them every week, and supporting the areas they need support in their lives. My two boys and their father are enjoying much father- son time together, and I thank God so much for this. For the grand turnaround. Thank you, Father God "Yahweh", in the name of our Savior Jesus Christ "Yeshua".

Reflection: Have you had struggles as a parent? Did you have support? If so, write down the support systems for which you're thankful. If you don't have support, release your hurt, and ask God to send good people into your life to support you and refine yourself. If you are considering becoming a parent, think of the people who will be there to support you as you start the journey of parenting. Make sure you take the time to get to know the person you will procreate with, and if you are second-guessing someone's behavior, that may not be a good person to have a child with. Also, if you've had a tough time while becoming a parent, have you had a turnaround? Have you had to balance your career while parenting? How can you get support to have balance so life can improve for you, your children, and your family? Write out your feelings about this subject as it pertains to your life.

Star K. Edwards

Star K. Edwards

Chapter VIII:

Refining My
Hardest Life Decision

While going through the things I'm speaking of in this book, especially around the time of becoming a mother, spiritual warfare hit me awfully hard. Many different people, especially the person I married, tried to destroy me. As I mentioned, when you are starting a relationship, you don't think you may be getting with a narcissistic, abusive person. They wear a mask and imitate the person they feel you want them to be, tricking you into believing you've found your soulmate. Sometimes you don't find out the type of person you are dealing with until you are fully invested in the relationship. I found out who I was dealing with after getting married and pregnant with my second son. Women are vulnerable people when pregnant, and some toxic people use that to their advantage. Good and healthy people will show love towards that woman as a child grows within them.

The abuse went to another level when I was in my most vulnerable state. Narcissists wait for the person they are targeting to be weak; that's when they take their abuse to the extreme. They want power and control over you while looking like they are wholesome people around others. They are demonic people who don't have a true relationship with God. Yes, some of them have gone to church and are in church. Some of them may show you the word of God, preach a message, and quote scriptures. But they don't know God. They deny Him and his power. As I mentioned, you will know them by their fruits and what they produce when others are not looking. They could look as if they are producing good Godly fruit, but you must become wise—as I have from my experiences—to pinpoint these people. I'm in my new awakening, especially after going through these experiences. I'm tapping into my gifts now, as well.

Going into my story for this chapter, I had to make the most major decision of my life, and that was...should I live? After the previous experiences, I now knew the evil of the world. I lived it, heard about it, and have seen it, but now I have experienced it on many levels. I had never really noticed the racism before as well pertaining to me personally. Being a good person and giving your love only to have them try to destroy you without a cause or explanation is the most hurtful thing. The narcissist I married told me to self-conclude myself so he could take the children. He encouraged this when I was in my deepest depression. He had a smirk on his face but was dead serious. While deeply depressed from his abuse and other unhealed wounds, I told him I would do it, and he encouraged me. He was straightforward and definitely sincere. I'm just glad I stayed strong and did not snap. I would never be led to do something like this because I know who my Father in heaven is and He has me in His Hands.

There are people who have self-concluded due to narcissistic abuse and the other things I mentioned in these chapters. I have seen the stories and studied this narcissistic personality disorder and its abuse every week for the last six, going on seven years, becoming aware of what was happening and what I was dealing with. Only people who have experienced this type of abuse would know what I'm talking about.

The narcissist never answered my question about why he hated me so much. I only asked that he be responsible and keep the promises he made, especially since it affected three people's lives tremendously. When I was affected, it affected my children. I had to fight hard for them not to see me in pain. I wanted him to be sympathetic to this, but he and his mother and family were not sympathetic. I married into a highly dysfunctional family who pretended to know God but didn't. As I mentioned before, the Bible says you will know them by their fruits. I wanted my children to have good people to turn to, but they do not have that with his family. I will show them the difference between healthy and toxic people, people of God and people not of God. Also, people attempting to live holy and upright. I will show them that I overcame many obstacles and refined my life and also had to learn to live upright.

I've been the levelheaded one of my children's two parents, but it took so much to get here—knowledge, wisdom, and a lot of work on myself. Also, we must know that good people are primarily targeted for narcissistic abuse. There are many reasons for this, which I plan to discuss in my next book. Narcissists mostly target good, kind, and empathic people. They love people who are empaths because we give so many chances and see the good in people, even if they or others don't see it. We don't want to leave if we see someone hurting and needing healing. At the same time, we need to focus on healing ourselves, which is what I have done. I've gone through a lot of healing through many resources, therapy, prayer and being more into the Word of God and more. Also, if you are one of the many people in the world who needs some healing, chances are you will be easily targeted for narcissistic abuse. Finally, if you are around familiar narcissistic spirits in your family, you will become an easy target for them.

I'm not going to change who I am because of narcissists and other toxic, evil people. I have the sense of awareness and wisdom now to avoid them. I also pray for people who are like this. I must also mention that some people believe you are an easy target if you're nice and kind. Those who are kind are actually the strong ones. People think my kindness is a weakness, but in actuality, it's a strength. In the last days, things that are good will seem bad, and things that are bad will seem good.

Don't get me wrong; I can get feisty and show another side once people cross the line with me too many times. I'm very patient and observe things before letting the feisty side out. However, I don't give too many chances now since I've come into knowledge and wisdom. The narcissist and his family were unable to destroy me; the enemy was not successful in using them to cause me harm. This situation just brought me an awareness of the true evil of this world. At the end of it all, evil will be destroyed!

Sometimes when a person has a major calling on their life, the enemy—Satan—tries to send the people who follow him to destroy good people. When I decided I would live for my children and fight through my circumstances, I took two trips to Paris, France, in 2018 for a highly spiritual service with beautiful African followers of Christ whose services were highly in tune with the Holy Spirit. I was consecrated and had a spiritual experience with God where I was filled with His spirit like I had never been before. I was even lifted off the ground. I felt God's presence; it was a heavenly experience and serene. I was not within myself. This was proof of the spiritual realm and that God is real. It is hard to explain the full spiritual experience, but it helped me to know for sure our God is real. This was the start of me refining my being and starting a new relationship with our Heavenly Father and His son, the true Jesus Christ. After this experience, I still fell as a human being, but God kept reminding me of who He is. I'm hoping those of you who are reading my story will be inspired and help inspire others. I want you all to see what God has brought me through, and still, I'm able to shine through it all! God is blessing my sons and me tremendously. He has His hands on us! God has refined and defined my life. It was only He who has gotten me through it all!

I asked for my ex to be responsible, and in return at that particular time, what I received was him wanting me to conclude, even if it included self-conclusion. The spirit within him wanted this. I have heard and witnessed relatable and comparable stories of other people who have been through remarkably similar situations. We must know that this world is of good and evil and we have a choice on what and who we shall choose between the two. We are wrestling against spirits within people and not the actual person. We are in a fallen world, and during these recent years, I've met people in situation-ships (not relationships) with people with dark spirits. There are a lot of people like this walking among us. These types of beings will not change me; don't allow them to change you, either. I will continue to show the love of God and pray for myself, my family, and others for us to walk upright. We should also pray for those who are lost. I eventually made a strong decision that I would get through these circumstances and break the chains of what was holding me down. I fought hard for my life, my children's lives, and future generations.

If you are a toxic person reading this, I encourage you to ask God into your heart and to invite his son, Jesus, into your life as your Lord and Savior, the true Lord and Savior. He is a forgiving God. He is also what kept me through it all!

Reflection: Think of a time when you had to make a life-altering decision. How did you stay strong? What are some things you need to heal from and release? Are there any people you need to forgive or work on forgiving? Jot down your answers and the names of the people. Also, write your prayer to God, asking him to strengthen and refine you after the pain and hurt. You will live, and you will live a Refined Life!

Star K. Edwards

Star K. Edwards

_____

_____

_____

_____

_____

_____

_____

_____

_____

_____

_____

_____

_____

_____

_____

_____

_____

Chapter IX:

Refining Myself Throughout the Pandemic—Hypocrisy of Country, Race, Culture, and Spirituality

In 2019 going into 2020, we started living in a worldwide pandemic with the virus COVID-19, which took the lives of millions of people. It had devastating effects on the world. One day, I was working while my little ones were in preschool; the next day, we were locked down at home. A stay-at-home order was put in place for the next year and a half. The state of California had one of the longest lockdowns in the country. Only essential places—such as supermarkets, pharmacies, and hospitals—were open. Schools were closed; courts were closed. About all places were closed. The virus spread so rapidly that we couldn't be around other people for over a year. My children and I stayed secluded in our home. I was anxious, and this pandemic was a good reason to put a person in full anxiety. I communicated daily with my family and close friends via phone, but I wished I had a husband with me during this time to comfort the children and me.

Unfortunately, I got COVID when our state started gradually opening up after eighteen months. My children had to fend for themselves somewhat because I had COVID so badly that I was in bed for over two weeks. They were brave to be little guys, though. Their father and my mother brought us hot food and left it outside the door since they couldn't come inside and risk catching the life-threatening and life altering virus. COVID caused me to be short-winded whenever I would get out of bed, but I survived. Once I was better, I tested my children and found they had caught COVID, as well, but did not have any major symptoms. My one son's symptoms only lasted for about a day.

My children were three and five years old when the pandemic lockdown started. It was a challenging time for me, parenting young children without help during the pandemic. It became exceedingly difficult not to have a break from parenting during COVID-19. The children's father became less abusive because he knew his manipulative tactics were no longer working on me. Thanks to the weekly narcissist abuse support videos I found on YouTube that shared the stories of other survivors, I became an expert on these types of individuals and how to deal with them. I no longer reacted to his tactics. He knew I was learning about people like him because when he would visit, I always had one of the narcissist informational YouTube videos playing. He eventually started taking more responsibility and became very consistent in talking to the children daily and spending time with them every weekend. Although I felt uncomfortable around him, I was glad he would come to see his children every week. Sure, I got a little break on the weekends, but not fully because he would visit them at my home. I had to do this so my children would be in a safe environment while seeing their father.

See, he lives with his mother and brother who are not safe people, and I did not know it at first. His mother had a lot to do with why he was not taking responsibility for being a husband and tried to stop him from being a father. Insane, right? I always thought it was men teaching children to become lousy adults, but another shocking revelation was finding out that toxic and narcissistic mothers led their tribe of children to become bad people. She even told her son not to take care of his first-born daughter, who he fathered when he was a young man. But this is a story for another time.

Back to what I was saying. So, during the pandemic, I only had a chance to rest when he came to see the children. I didn't start feeling comfortable enough for him to take them on short trips to the store until a year or so later, mostly months after the pandemic passed. I also started hiring babysitters and housekeepers to help me out around the house. It freed up some of my time so I could focus on creating my legacy and for me to rest. If you are someone who doesn't have a support system to help you at times, then it would be best for you to hire outside help, which is what I did and continue to do.

While stuck in the house during the pandemic, I watched *CNN World News* daily. I should've turned the TV off because I started getting extreme anxiety from hearing about all the people dying from COVID. It reminded me of the 1919 flu pandemic. The documentaries were shown to remind us of what happened and that we are living in similar times. Months after being at home, I tried to go and stay with my family. It was a little toxic, but eventually, the boys and I visited for a few weeks with my sister Jessica and her girls. I was glad to be with my family and spend time with my sister and nieces. After having to be inside for so long and not being around people, I started experiencing the worst panic attacks and anxiety attacks of my life. They were so bad that I couldn't even get behind the wheel of my car to drive. My UCLA community was there to help me do breathing exercises. We were all in this together.

At this time, I started reading my bible more and rededicated my life to the Lord. Afraid of what was happening, I started being on prayer lines, being in the Word, and having a closer relationship with God. Before doing this, it was the worst time for my mental health. I had never experienced gradually feeling unattached and blacking out. Many others were enduring the same mental health issues during this time, and we were in a worldwide mental health crisis due to the pandemic. It was in the news that people who never had mental health issues were and are now experiencing it, and others who did have issues were getting worse. I asked God to please bring me through this and I will strive wholeheartedly to follow His Word and help to bring others to Him. Before the pandemic and before re-dedicating my life back to Christ and Refining My Being, I had gotten back into acting and arts for this was for me to be back uplifted from my atrocities and to start back doing what I love. So, before the pandemic and before rededicating my life back to Christ, I was offered to be in a film in which I was told I would be playing a classy character. I eventually accepted the offer to be in a love scene, but with no nudity and I thought it would be a quick scene. I didn't fully know that the movie was not of God, until I saw the final product. I had not fully indulged myself into the whole script and the movie turned out to be what I did not expect on many levels. The film did not represent me or what my Refined Life or my Refined Being is about, even though it may just be acting. I have to represent my God at all times. I know I am only human and there are times I will still fall, but there are things I know better now as well. I am a Refined Being and moving forward as I re-dedicate myself back to the Lord, I now represent God as His Daughter and someone who helps bring the lost to Him, not helping people stay lost and not encouraging people to go astray. I also want to lead people out of the darkness to not focus on sex, promiscuity, drugs, lack of family and I do not condone these sins to be focused on especially culturally through the media, unless it is sending a message of change for the good and the better of one's being. It only continues to hurt people and future offspring to have this type of art and lifestyle as what's exciting, when it only gradually destroys a person, a community, a culture, and a people. There needs to be a change regarding this. I now ask you Father God for forgiveness when I had not represented you better in the arts at all times and not being aware of the full and final message of a project. Moving forward I now represent you as I am yours and you are my Heavenly Father. I want to be pleasing to you God and what I do to be pleasing in your sight and to lead others to You Father God, In the Name of Jesus Christ Our Lord, Amen, Amen and Amen!!!

Another issue that led to mental health problems during the pandemic was watching the daily news of the U.S. president at the time. We were in a racial crisis due to his presidency. His presidency was mainly a backlash from the U.S. having the 1st African American president, who was well-liked and admired worldwide, including his family. I was so happy to have been a community organizer and worked on his presidential campaign, helping to make history. The world was now seeing positive images of a Black man or melanated man, his family, brilliance, intelligence, etc. It was the opposite of the negative images the media systematically focuses on, mainly showing people of color doing terrible things and purposely not showing them acting positively and being extraordinary geniuses. This is to keep everyone's minds falsely believing that one set of people is perfect and does only good. There are people who do low life actions in all cultures and backgrounds, including backgrounds of people who have a lighter beige appearance. Low-life actions include rape, abuse, stealing, etc.

People strive for excellence in all cultures, including so-called Black people, people of brown appearance (melanin people), negroes, or people of color. Cultural educator Jane Elliot mentioned that Black people are mostly not the actual color black. Most are brown and come in shades of chestnut, tan, red, etc. She said to pull a crayon out of a crayon box and compare your skin with the color of the crayon; most so-called blacks' skin is actually bronze in color or the color brown. The term Black is purposely used negatively, and in the dictionary, it purposely has negative definitions of black things and should not define a group of people all in one category as the same or in a negative light. Also, as spiritual beings, we are based on having a bright or dark spirit no matter the outer human appearance. Regarding the outer human shell, God made a rainbow full of beautiful colors of people from the lightest to the darkest from all nations. He made the world not boring, but beautiful and colorful to have not just one type of skin tone. Finally, like Jane Elliot, a woman of European descent, doesn't mention the term Black regarding people in a negative way, but a positive way. The skin is melanin, and melanin is a good thing—being kissed by the sun.

Hateful hearted people did not want to see the great images of the first African American president and hated that the first African American presidency went on for eight years. Race issues were always a problem, but during the pandemic, the hate and evil of people were now spotlighted. People started feeling as if their privilege would be taken away and the evil that they and their ancestors had done to people would come back to them. People of darker skin being in power was becoming a threat to the so-called privileged. This became a battle for America during the pandemic. This caused more chaos while people continued to perish from COVID.

It was time to find out about the many historical lies which have been buried, including Jesus not looking as if he was European but having dark skin—which was more of a dark-brown bronzy color. I learned there are two types of real and false representations of Christ. One of love and one of hate. The one of hate is the false one. Many things which created privileged people were based on false narratives and lies. Many hidden truths came about during this time, and people are fighting to keep these truths buried.

During COVID, I was surprised people didn't show more love to one another. People were losing loved ones and hearing of others who have. I thought the world would grow closer to God. I thought people would get their spiritual life together. I, myself, decided to rededicate, recommit and to get my life right with Christ during this time and others did as well. Some people just continued their hate and evil. I was shocked to find out about racism in the white evangelical church. As I mentioned, the real Jesus Christ is of love, not of hate. His primary commandment was to love one another, including people of all nationalities and cultures. He made us all. God said do not worry about these types of people who try to hurt others because he will avenge his true people and the oppressed—even in the afterlife—because we are spiritual beings who will transition from the human experience, which is guaranteed for every person.

I urge you, my readers, to have love in your hearts for one another. The word of God, the living holy word, speaks of "what profits a man to gain the whole world but lose his soul." To gain worldly power and privilege is not a great profit if a person does all of this but loses his soul in the process. We all should want to prepare to hear from the Creator God, our Father, to say, "Well done, my son and daughter." These are the words I want to hear from Yahweh, my God, my Father, and His son Yeshua Jesus.

Reflection: Think of the time of the worldwide pandemic. How did you stay strong? What were some of the obstacles you faced? How was your mental health? How was your physical health? Write a prayer to God thanking him for your and your family's survival during COVID-19. If you lost a loved one during this time, ask God to strengthen you. Ask God and the faithful Lord Jesus Christ into your life if you don't know Him. Write whatever comes to your mind pertaining to this topic. Remember, He wants us to draw closer to Him. He will help you refine your being.

Star K. Edwards

Chapter X:

Refining a Brand-New Me; Love, Light, & More God

In this concluding chapter, I will speak of being a brand-new me. Some people may say I've never experienced the things others have experienced to this extreme. There are various reasons some people experience more than others. Sometimes when you have a great calling on your life, being anointed and chosen, the spiritual enemy will focus on you and use other people to try and destroy you. I'm here to tell the people who may have lost hope to look at my life. I've overcome so much and know deep down in my spirit that Father God has brought me through. He never left me or forsaken me. We just live in a fallen world and must learn how to maneuver in it while being aware that we are wrestling not against flesh and blood but principalities in the spiritual realm.

As I mentioned in this book, we are spiritual beings having a human experience. There are people who allow the spiritual enemy to use them to fight against what's good or working towards well. Ephesians 6:11-24 in the Holy Word of God says, *"Put on the whole armor of God, that ye may be able to stand against the wiles of the devil. For we wrestle not against flesh and blood, but against principalities, against powers, against the rulers of the darkness of this world, against spiritual wickedness in high places. Wherefore take unto you the whole armor of God, that ye may be able to withstand in the evil day, and having done all, to stand. Stand therefore, having your loins girt about with truth, and having on the breastplate of righteousness; And your feet shod with the preparation of the gospel of peace; Above all, taking the shield of faith, wherewith ye shall be able to quench all the fiery darts of the wicked. And take the helmet of salvation, and the sword of the Spirit, which is the word of God: Praying always with all prayer and supplication in the Spirit, and watching thereunto with all perseverance and supplication for all saints; And for me, that utterance may be given unto me, that I may open my mouth boldly, to make known the mystery of the gospel, For which I am an ambassador in bonds: that therein I may speak boldly, as I ought to speak. But that ye also may know my affairs, and how I do, Tychicus, a beloved brother and faithful minister in the Lord, shall make known to you all things: Whom I have sent unto you for the same purpose, that ye might know our affairs, and that he might comfort your hearts. Peace be to the brethren, and love with faith, from God the Father and the Lord Jesus Christ. Grace be with all of them that love our Lord Jesus Christ in sincerity. Amen."*

This verse describes the spiritual battle that exists in the lives of believers. It does so better than any other words in Scripture. First, it affirms our battle is indeed spiritual, not physical. The enemies we face, ultimately, are not people or objects. The devil may use those as part of his attack, but our true opponent is not other people––it is sin. Second, it identifies our spiritual enemies. This list is commonly interpreted as a vague listing of the "ranks" within the demonic armies. "Rulers" seem to indicate a top level of evil spiritual forces. "Authorities" refer to general forces of evil attacking believers. "Cosmic powers" seems to refer to the worldwide nature of this spiritual battle. "Evil in the spiritual places" again emphasizes a battle beyond this world.

Spiritual battles can occur at all levels, anywhere across this world and beyond with human beings. The believer must be prepared for all types of attacks by putting on God's armor, as it describes. This is what I've fought through these chapters of my life—many spiritual battles. I now know how to put on the whole armor of God. I'm glad because I've always known who God was and have accepted His son, Jesus Christ. I was able to rely on Him and keep my faith and hope in Him as much as possible. The Lord has never left nor forsaken me in this fallen world and my situations.

In these situations, I have gone through the refining process. Refining is the process of purification of a substance or a form. It's to be free from impurities or unwanted material, to be free from moral imperfection, and to elevate and improve or perfect by pruning or polishing. I have been pruned and polished. There was a time when I focused more on my flesh and my spirit started to feel empty and when I focus on feeding my spirit with the Word of God, then my flesh doesn't feel like it needs to be fed, because I'm feeding it with the Spirit of God. The flesh and doing fleshy things take a human being from feeling the Spirit of God, and I want to continuously feel more of my Father God. Also in my life, people being used by the enemy have tried to destroy me, but it's also because I stayed in their presence too long. In the past, I tried to overly please people thinking it would make them happy and I thought we could live peacefully with one another. If they exploded for no reason, I would work harder to try and appease them. I no longer take on individuals' projected pain. I no longer walk on eggshells and am not responsible for anyone's triggers and malignancy. I focus now on myself and most importantly, my children. I am no longer depleting myself due to someone else's toxicity. I maintain healthy boundaries, especially with those who are unhealthy. I learned that some people will never like me because my spirit irritates their demons.

I didn't know these things or who I was when I was in the rough. While going through the refinement process and adversities, I gradually gained new knowledge and wisdom. By the grace of God, I have persevered through some circumstances that many people are unable to come out of. I went from being fragmented to becoming one of fullness, wholeness, and boldness. I have learned these major lessons and have moved to higher grounds with God's glory, and His glory shines through me!

The word of God says in due season, we will be exalted if we faint not. I have not fainted. I have persevered, and He gave me the strength never to give up. He has covered me and my children. I now have a new vision—a new way of looking at things with much wisdom. I would never go back to my old life. I will no longer give myself to toxic people or any fools. I will focus on what pleases my Father God "Yahweh." Some people are missing something inside them, showing jealousy and malice because they feel you have something they don't. This leads to a spirit within them that wants to destroy a person because of this, as well. If only everyone realized that they can tap into their gifts and have an opportunity to bring good to the world. I will pray for those who are lost, but will no longer associate with toxic people and ungodly people who feel the need to destroy others to deplete them in order to feel a sense of satisfaction from it. I pray for, encourage, and inspire others as much as I can, and it is up to people whether they will receive it. My problem was staying too long in the midst of destructive individuals who were controllers, manipulators, gaslighters, narcissists, etc. At the first sign of anyone having a toxic personality, I immediately disengage and block those types of spirits. I engage with people who are of love and goodness. We should all be striving to be more of this. More like the true living Christ Jesus who died for our sins so we can connect to our Father God, our Creator, and have eternal life to dwell with him someday in eternity. I also ask God again to please forgive me for stepping out of his will for my life. Anything I have done that is not of my heavenly Father God, before writing this book, I ask for His full forgiveness in the name of Jesus.

I am now refined into a new being and walking in my purpose. I was in the refiner's fire for an exceedingly long time but came out winning, soaring, and shining. I became refined, free of impurities, evolved, and pushed up to higher heights. You, too, can refine yourself. Whatever people may have thought of you negatively can be changed. You don't have to wear the label of what you used to be or what you have done. You can be refined in the Creator or God "Yahweh" in the name of Jesus "Yeshua." People thought they were drowning me, but instead, I was being cleansed. I have a newfound awareness, and you can, as well. I'm an advocate of all things right and good. I have shared my story in hopes of opening up opportunities for others to tell their stories that will inspire and change lives.

When you see me happy, enjoying life, traveling the world, using my gifts of relating to people culturally, and more, look back at my story and remember what God has brought me through. God has illuminated my soul and raised me onto the mountaintop. His glory is radiating through my soul! I had to learn how to be whole. I needed to heal childhood wounds and more wounds from my adult years until I finally cried out to God, and He showed me how to get out of the cycle and what the familiar spirits were. He showed me who I was in Him. It took so much to get to that place, but I have finally awakened and shifted to a place of wholeness and boldness. There is no turning back. I am now walking in my power. I've come a long way to now living out my dreams and purpose. I have freedom. I also have forgiven those who caused so much pain and who have tremendously hurt me. I am free as well for not forgetting, but because I have forgiven them. This has been hard, but this is what God has called me and has called for us to do. I'm renewed, and I can breathe. I now have more of God, giving Him the time and glory. I'm no longer giving my energy, time, gifts, or purpose to people who are set on trying to destroy and who are being used by the enemy. Again, I now have more of God and am giving Him the time and glory! I glorify His name. The Lord Thy God shall be exalted! I thank you, Father God, for saving me and protecting my children, my loved ones, and myself. This book is a part of breaking the chains and to demolish the cycle of inflicted causes to defeat and prevail for my children and for generations to come! This vicious cycle is destroyed, and there's no turning back. What the enemy meant for evil, my Almighty God turned it around for my good. I went through so much to tell my story, so God will get the Glory! I am a Refined Being! Amen!!!

Reflection: Has your understanding of how God refines you changed? If you are currently in a refining process, what negative elements have risen to the top (things you are now aware of) that need to be removed? What was your reaction to these things when they were revealed? Write down the steps you'll do starting today to renew your mind, body, and spirit so you can become a "Refined Being" and come out shining like God's diamond.

Star K. Edwards

_____

_____

_____

_____

_____

_____

_____

_____

_____

_____

_____

_____

_____

_____

_____

_____

_____

HALLELUJAH! PRAISE GOD FROM HEAVEN, PRAISE HIM FROM THE MOUNTAINTOPS; PRAISE HIM, ALL YOU HIS ANGELS, PRAISE HIM, ALL YOU HIS WARRIORS, PRAISE HIM, SUN AND MOON, PRAISE HIM, YOU MORNING STARS; PRAISE HIM, HIGH HEAVEN, PRAISE HIM, HEAVENLY RAIN CLOUDS; PRAISE, OH LET THEM (US) PRAISE THE NAME OF GOD-HE SPOKE THE WORD, AND THERE THEY WERE! HE SET THEM IN PLACE FROM ALL TIME TO ETERNITY; HE GAVE HIS ORDERS, AND THAT'S IT!

PSALMS 148: 1-6

Extra Self-Reflection Note Pages

**For My Readers to Reflect on Your Own Story
& For You to Also Become a Refined Being**